# REAL LOVE

STRATEGIES FOR REACHING STUDENTS WHEN
THEY SEE NO WAY OUT

ALEXES M. TERRY

EduMatch Publishing

# CONTENTS

# DEDICATION

*First and foremost, I would like to thank God for this book and for giving me the strength and vision behind this book. Thank you to my amazing husband-- Zachary Terry--and my children Brandon, Anthony, Hannah, and Benjamin for supporting me and being patient with me during the writing process. I hope that you guys see that you can do ANYTHING despite facing obstacles in life. I love you, and I am so honored to be your wifey and mommy. To my mom, dad, stepmom, and siblings...THANK YOU! Life has ups and downs, and my story would not be what it is without your stories. Thank you for always supporting me even when we do not always see eye to eye. I love you guys, and I am constantly cheering for you guys.*

*Each of you have powerful testimonies, and I enjoy seeing how God is/will use your lives to transform the lives of others. Uncle Anthony, your "girl" did it, and thank you for always having my back and cheering me on. Thank you to Mrs. McDow, Mr. Conard, Ms. Hyde, and all of the educators who invested in me even when I did not feel worthy of your investment. Because of your work and your example, REAL LOVE is possible. Lastly, and most importantly, Grandma Jeweleen and Uncle Benny, thank you for laying down your lives so that I could live and dream. Thank you for your constant support, love, and encouragement. I miss you guys so much, but I find comfort in knowing that I did exactly what you guys wanted me to do--get an education and go after my dreams. I hate that you guys are not here to witness this moment, but I know that you are watching from heaven with the biggest smiles on your faces. I cannot thank you enough, so I'll just continue to press forward. To my nieces and nephews, students, and all the kids in the "hood," do not let anyone tell you what you can't do. In the words of the late Nipsey Hussle, "the marathon continues."*

# INTRODUCTION

---

"Education Is Not The Filling Of A Pail But The Lightening Of A Fire."

-WB YEATS

---

Teachers possess the power to change the world or at least the way someone sees the world. I understand the transformative power of teaching because, like many educators out there, a teacher transformed my life. Talk to any educator, and they can share a story about that one teacher who captured their hearts and reeled them in with real love. Not only did they create a passion for learning, but they also created a desire in us to make others feel the way they made us feel.

Unfortunately, the reality of public education has caused the flame in many educators to dwindle. Many of these educators teach in old and failing schools in the inner cities of America. The schools, teachers, and students have little hope. As a result, good teachers are leaving the profession, and urban youth are being passed along without the skills and tools needed to compete in our ever-changing society. Alternatively, we lose them to the streets--gangs, crime, drugs, jail, or ultimately death. What hurts the most is to see the disregard that some educators have for students who exist in urban schools or come from urban communities. In learning spaces, these students are often marginalized or tossed to the side as if they have nothing to offer the greater good of our nation, society, or this world. Kids from the streets have potential and possess skills and social capital unimaginable to some educators. They possess an inner light that, for some, shines bright while the darkness that surrounds them dimmed the light of others. When these students enter our buildings, they want to shine, but struggle with turning that light back on. They are in a constant search for something to make them whole again; hope to believe that their current situation is a temporary part of this journey called life. In this quest, what they are looking for is REAL LOVE; the agape kind of love that is true, consistent, and never failing. They are looking for educators who can extend to them this kind of love; those who are excited about EVERY student they encounter--being there and ready to connect with them on a personal and more profound level. They are waiting for someone to grab hold of them and bring them in and out of the dark. They are looking for a person who will show them a light at the end of the tunnel if they allow their hearts to hold on.

I know this because I was one of those students. By the time I made it to my adolescent years, the streets of South Central, Los Angeles, and the things I witnessed daily had sucked all hope out of me. The years in elementary, middle, and high school were a full-blown search for REAL LOVE. What I hoped to find was someone to help me add meaning to my life. The love I received in the home was questionable, so I went to find it elsewhere. When I entered the halls of the school, I turned on this internal flashlight inside of me and went on this quest. From one classroom to another, I searched for who or what I could love in hopes that they would love me back. When I did not find it in the schools, I walked right out the front gate, or hopped the back fence, and went into the streets looking for love elsewhere.

To my fortune, the streets have taught me a lot about the classroom and how to reach students when they see no way out. This book serves as my advice to all educators. It is also a guide to transforming the environment of urban schools in hopes of transforming the lives of students. We have lost too many students to the streets because they cannot find the love and connection they seek at home or in our schools. If we do not welcome them in our schools and show them that they are loved, the mean streets of some of the toughest inner cities will do so with open arms. As educators, we can end this cycle of losing students to gangs, drugs, crime, and jail, but we must first transform the way students in urban communities do and experience learning in our schools. We can save countless lives and restore lost souls. The strategy to do so is showing every student R.E.A.L. L.O.V.E.

Throughout this book, I will use my personal stories, professional experiences, and knowledge of Culturally Relevant/Responsive pedagogy, Reality pedagogy, and social-emotional learning (because SEL is foundational to effective Culturally Responsive Teaching) to break down the acronym R.E.A.L. L.O.V.E. The nucleus of this concept is meeting students where they are, creating individualized learning experiences that are relevant to their lives and important to their cultural values and communities, and helping them actualize the potential that they already possess. R.E.A.L. L.O.V.E. is not meant to be catchy, but a call to action. It is also not meant to be the final solution as I still have more growing and learning to do as an educator and human being. To be honest, writing this book is my way of making sense of my childhood, educational experiences, and answering a question that I get asked often: how did I get to where I am today despite my upbringing. At the end of this read, I want each educator that turns the pages of this book to evaluate their approaches to teaching and learning and reconsider any practices that might be oppressive, racist, or undermining their students' actual potential. I want to motivate educators to transform the experiences and opportunities they create in their classrooms and schools for their students. But I also want to hold educators accountable for taking the steps necessary to create a learning environment where all students have the opportunity to succeed despite their race, class, abilities, or zip code. In the end, I want educators to understand that true equity in education starts in our classrooms and schools. Every student has the potential to be successful in life. Our duty is to help them define what success looks like to them and walk alongside them as they transcend odds and walk into a future full of opportunities. Yes, for every student, this is possible. But, again, it starts with us. In our classrooms and schools, we have to commit to getting real with our students, no matter how hard it may get, and love them in a way that will transform the way they view themselves, their families, their schools, their communities, and their potential.

# ONE

# RELATIONSHIPS WITH STUDENTS
## ROOTED IN RESPECT

---

*"The gangs filled a void in society, and the void was the absence of family life. The gang became a family. For some of those guys in the gang that was the only family they knew, because when their mothers had them, they were too busy having children for other men. Some of them never knew their daddies. Their daddies never looked back after they got their mothers pregnant, and those guys just grew up, and they couldn't relate to nobody."*

GEORGE MACKEY

---

I felt so pretty on that hot day in June of 2000. The day barely came, but it was exciting to be there. Looking around at all of the faces of friends, we were excited to be at that moment. Looking at the faces of the family there to support--dad, grandma, and uncle--they grinned from ear to ear with pride. My mother did not do it, my father did not do it, and my oldest brother did not do it. I barely made it, but I did it. I jumped out of my seat when I heard my name called. Wait! What is this? I thought to myself. "And the award for *The Most Improved Student* goes to Alexis Toomes." That is correct, "Most Improved Student" for Henry Clay Middle School's Class of 2000.

I grew up rough. By the time I graduated from the eighth grade, I knew more about crack rocks, shoplifting, and gang banging than I knew about the "Three Rs"--reading, writing, and arithmetic. I was a product of the streets of South Central, Los Angeles. My mother was a crack addict, and my father was still trying to figure out his life--sober and gang-affiliated. I had my grandmother and uncles, who took the place of my mother and father. Like many in my neighborhood, I was trying to figure out where I could fit in. I also needed to know who was going to have my back in streets that remained dangerous.

Similar to many inner cities, gangs were prevalent. In my neighborhood, having friends who graduated and went to college was an anomaly. If one of my friends did make it to their high school graduation, their very next move was to get out of South Central, find work that only required minimum skills and a high school diploma, or be immediately jumped into a gang or get initiated into a clique. Now, a few of my friends made it out of L.A., but someone had to grab hold of them quickly, take them under the wing and help them get out and escape falling for the gang culture. Gang culture in my "hood"--the Rolling 100s-- was more prominent than just representing a color, street, or a side of town. Gangs were family and gangbangers were real friends, especially when all of the family members and family friends a person had likely made up the gangs that surrounded their neighborhood. Gangbanging was the thing to do, and when it came to a family bond, that was all some of us knew. That shared experiences and identities is what made gangs desirable, and because we did not know where we belonged, being a "gangsta" seemed like the best alternative.

What makes the gang life and street life so appealing are the relationships one has and a sense of respect one gained from being associated with a street gang or clique. Some of the fellow "homies" have been by your side since childhood. Others welcomed new initiates into the hood with open arms. This welcome is contingent on the willingness to be down for their cause and their hood. However, it was a welcome that some needed to feel valued and significant. Once a person was "put on," you became a part of something bigger. Something that felt real when everything else that existed was questionable. The love a person could not find in the home or the school developed with their "hood." More than likely, before considering gang life, a cry for love was heard. It echoed through classrooms and the halls of the school. Instead of capturing the heart, that heart rerouted in another direction on its quest for love.

In order to connect with students, from any race, culture, or background, a relationship is a must. However, this relationship must be rooted in respect. When seeking to develop authentic relationships with our students, we must not only be interested in the surface parts of them, but we must show sincere interest in everything that makes them who they are. Their communities, their cultures, and their passions must be of interest to us as well, and just like we seek to get to know a student, we must also seek to develop a respect and appreciation for all they hold near and dear to their hearts.

## Connections Over Content

I will never forget the conversations that were taking place in the teacher's lounge during in-service, after my former principal instructed all teachers to halt instruction for the first two weeks of school and spend time getting to know every student. I thought this was a great idea, especially considering the urban school we were in and the demographics of students. However, this idea was not popular among my colleagues. "I have so much stuff to teach that I cannot risk that much time," one teacher scoffed. Another felt "two weeks was too much time trying to get to know some kids. All I need is a day or two, but I have to get into teaching!" I was excited about the idea of quality bonding time, especially when we had permission from above to put connections over the content.

Our students are like different subjects to us. Before we journey into the unknown, we do our research. Before we let a person into our home, we get to know them. Thorough background checks take place before we are even trusted to receive clearance into a place of importance. Well, how is it that we expect students to feel welcomed in our environments and trust us with cultivating their minds when we will not even take more than two hours to start investing in a relationship with them? In the words of multicultural educator Gary Howard (2016), "we cannot teach what we do not know," and our students will not learn from someone they do not know, respect or trust. They may retain a certain amount of content, but "real learning" is not taking place.

During my middle school years, I was a real class act mainly because I was acting out. My mother was on the streets looking for her next high, my grandmother was continually working to support three more kids after raising her own seven, and my dad was trying to make sense of his new life post addiction. I had friends in school, but no real connections because I was too scared that someday they would come to my house, see my mother sleeping in her box on the porch to sober up, and then the world would know I was the daughter of a crackhead. The relationships that I did have were all based on my fears. They also filled voids for what I did not have at home. I had a play momma, play dad, and a host of play sisters and play brothers, but none of them were my real friends because they did not know the real me. I did not know the real me and would push anyone away who tried to get to know the real me. I spent more time skipping class than in class because of fears and insecurities. However, what did it matter? No one knew or cared that I was gone, and when I did show up to class, it felt like every teacher was looking for the fastest way to get me out. My oldest brother was already the menace of the school and got expelled. I guess I was just like him, and not one educator made me feel any different.

I spent a lot of my time during middle school in in-school suspension (ISS). While I cannot remember the ISS teacher's name, I will never forget the way she made me feel. ISS back then was not what it is like today. When you went to the ISS room, you did not go with tons of busywork.

Most times, the teacher did not even care to send any work. My brother was already popular and had made a name for himself, so the ISS teachers were very familiar with who I was. I spent much of the time in this room talking. Even when I was not supposed to be in ISS, I spent my time in ISS. Not because of the place but because of the people--or one woman in particular. Because I longed for a maternal figure, I did one of two things when it came to women. I either pushed them away or clung tight to them. In the ISS room, I found someone I could cling on to tightly.

Mrs. Jacobs, the lead ISS teacher, reminded me of my grandmother, but her "take no crap" attitude made me wish she was my mother. Since there was no content being taught in that room, connections developed. Every day that I had to serve was another day for her to get to know and understand me. She would ask questions, give compliments, and help me identify my strengths. She wanted to know about my family, my likes and dreams, and she often told me stories about her family and her life. In her presence, I did not feel a burden and did not feel like I was a burden. I did not feel like I was being judged or compared to the likeliness of my oldest brother. Her interest in me was genuine, and I knew it. Because she knew me, she was able to see past the labels that were placed on me at 12, and she planted a seed in my heart. The relationship we had was one of trust because she respected me, my family, and my community. Every day I went to the ISS room to talk or see if there was anything I could do to give her a hand. Because of the connection we had, I wanted to come back and file papers, clean the boards, or even wipe down the desk. Anything I could do to be in her space, I did it.

I can recall when my mother finally went to prison while pregnant with my younger brother. Ms. Jacobs was one of the first people on the campus that knew what I was experiencing on the inside. Others assumed that my mother was "out in the streets," but no campus personnel ever asked me about it or how it made me feel. However, she did. When she heard that I would sit out on the baseball field alone and cry, she sent for me, and from then on, I knew I was more than just a troubled student to her. I was never expected or pushed to be above average. As long as I was "passing," I was "okay," in the eyes of my guardians. However, she pushed and inspired me to seek to be more than average and told me I could be better than my mother, sister, or brother. She made me not want to disappoint her (and she told me I better not bring my butt back to ISS), and from that point on, I fought to be better, although it was still a daily struggle. It was her push that got me to my 8th grade graduation day (with Cs and Ds), and a time I will never forget.

It should NOT have taken a trip to the ISS room for an educator to stop and ask me, "what was up with [me]?" Intervention should have happened well before then. The sign of a troubled student was written all over me, but, in my eyes, no one cared enough to really stop, read, and reflectively judge the behavior I was displaying. We should know our students well enough--early on--to know when something is off about them. If we cannot get close to them, then we must make it our duty to develop a connection and relationship with them. They must become our one as we pursue establishing a lasting connection with them.

In my personal and professional career, I have seen teachers get so caught up in what they were teaching that they did not notice changes in the *whom* they were teaching. The content we teach and the priority we place on it can become about us if we are not careful. We enter this race to nowhere, at the beginning of the year, and we leave our students behind in the dust as they are still trying to decide if they should trust us or not. We should place value and emphasis on relationships rooted in respect because when a student knows that we have a genuine interest in their well-being and not just their academic success, the results will come. Their lives should be our priority as we emphasize our desire to pursue genuine connections over teaching content.

## You Gotta Keep It Fresh

When I think about building relationships with students, I think about old-fashion courting and connecting with a potential mate. You want to take the relationship slow and steady while taking the time to get to know each other. However, you also want to make sure that the excitement and newness of the relationship do not fade away on the slow course. When starting the "courting phase," we are on our "A-game" and seeking to play all of the cards right. We make sure to wear the right clothes, say the right things, and make the right moves to make sure we keep our potential mate coming back for more. To keep our mate interested, we make every effort to keep the relationship fresh, fun, and exciting. From the cute outfits to the spur of the moment and creative outings, we show out so they can continue to show up. Once they are ours, hopefully, we keep freshening things up in our relationships to show our significant others how worthy they are and essential to us. Because we want this relationship to last, we are careful with everything we do and do not do. Essential to any relationship that is going to last, we are patient in the "getting to know you" phase and slow to grow.

WHEN WE ARE ENGAGING students in relationship-building, it is not something that is going to happen overnight. Be slow to grow. While I encourage using the first couple of school days to focus only on cultivating relationships with students (not yourself, classroom rules and procedures, or syllabi), your effort to truly connect with them cannot be rushed and should not be rushed. It should also not be placed on the backburner once you get in the trenches. Also, we have to keep it fresh, even in the most stressful times. What made me genuinely open up and connect with my ISS teacher was the space and time she allowed for me to get to know her, and I knew she was her real self (which is something I will discuss later on). Every moment with her was refreshing and new. The time that she gave and the conversations we had were transformational. They allowed me to go to spaces where I forgot all that caused me to hurt. Ms. Jacobs often approached me from different angles and was skilled in using my cultural references to connect with me in a way that made me feel visible. She was intentional about finding out how to best connect with me and constantly switching up her methods to keep me listening to the lessons taught. The way to see and know our students for who they are, we must be relaxed, honest, transparent, and open-minded.

Most importantly, we must create an environment where they know they are valued, respected, and protected. The environment must seek to lift students and edify them, not one that makes them feel as if a weight fell on their shoulders as soon as they walk in the room. When students enter our classrooms, they can immediately tell what is of importance-- them or "your class." The start of each day should be devoted to connecting to our students in exciting new ways, and letting them know that we, too, are human. They should see the emotions we go through and how we, as adults and professionals, process and healthily handle those emotions. Each day should provide a creative spin to relationship building with your transparency reeling them in and wanting more of what you have to offer. My students have seen me excited, happy, mad, hurt, and frustrated. They have heard the countless, and appropriate, stories of the good and the bad. My testimony is something that I was once ashamed of, but now I use it in my classroom to show persistence and triumph. I have inspired many students with my personal story, but I am still chasing after a few.

Who we are as educators becomes evident through the relationships that we seek to build with our students. They can see the passion we have for them and for our profession through the connections we seek to develop. These connections can make a world of difference to who they are at that moment, and what they can become in the future. Nothing can guarantee that relationships will create a turnaround in some of our most troubling and lost students, but the possibilities are worth every moment spent getting real. Let us use every moment we have.

## It Does Not End at The Sound of The Bell

I close this chapter with the story of Bryan Edwards. Bryan was one of my very first students whom I would never forget. He taught me how to love and advocate for my students when they could not do it for themselves. He also taught me the power of building relationships. By the time Bryan made it to his junior year in high school, he was broken and beaten mentally and emotionally. At the age of 16, he was trying to "get in where he fit in." He was labeled as SPED, passed along, and made to feel like he was bothersome by many teachers he had encountered. To this day, I am not sure what it was about Bryan, but I went on a mission to help him see his light. However, I had to capture his heart first. Bryan did not know what success looked or felt like because his grades or assessment results always measured him. He did not get the interventions he needed to be successful because it was easier to pass him along rather than deal with him or the helicopter father he had for a parent. Bryan was a victim of Hurricane Katrina, and while he had been in Texas for some time, he was still missing and longing for what he knew as home. His body became synonymous with the images of the disregarded Katrina victims we often saw in the news. No one understood him because no one fully understood the trauma that he and his family experienced. No one understood his father's drive to provide his son with a better life, and education, because they did not like his aggressive tactics. He was a helicopter parent. However, Mr. Edwards was willing to do whatever it took to see his son graduate from high school and not become a statistic like many young African American males.

AS A NEW TEACHER, I had yet to encounter a student like Bryan. So, I interacted with him and his father the best way I knew how--with compassion. The same compassion I longed for from my teachers. What I saw in Bryan was someone who had known he was written off in school. He struggled in school and struggled to justify his struggle at home. He had given up because, on paper, he was already a failure. His smile told me differently. Bryan was on edge in his journey of self-identification. In many ways, he reminded me of myself at his age. From acting out in class, refusing to do assignments, to even experimenting with opioids in the school's bathroom, Bryan was crying out for help, but his voice became mute. I had to push myself, and other educators, to see Bryan for who he was and give him what his heart and mind needed--love and grace. Through in-class one-on-ones, hallway interactions, after-school tutorials, and some real momma love, Bryan and I developed a strong bond. It was not an easy one to develop because just when I thought I had him hooked, something else caught his attention. Bryan getting distracted happened again, and again, and again. I realized that my presence in his life and our connection had to be stronger. It had to be stronger than the forces in the streets that were pulling him away from the school.

After a long year of working, bonding, and encouraging Bryan, a significant breakthrough had come for Bryan's confidence. After years of never passing a standardized test, Bryan successfully passed the End-of-Course exam for my subject. This moment was big for him because it allowed him to see the potential he had inside of him. For me, this moment showed me the results of prioritizing my connections with a student over the content. Everyone wanted to know what "tricks" I used. As a brand-new teacher, I had no tricks. What I had was a relationship with a student where we both respected and genuinely loved each other. Bryan knew that despite what he did, I had his back, and I was one of his biggest supporters and advocates when it came to his academic success and overall well-being.

Bryan went on to graduate from high school and attend a local community college. However, sadly, once we parted ways, the forces of the streets had a stronger connection to him. I will never forget the call I received from his father about three years after Bryan had graduated, and I had moved on to a new school. He called me because gang life and drugs had consumed Bryan, and he was at the end of his rope. Doing all that a father could for his son, but running out of options, Mr. Edwards called me--the one person could reel Bryan back in and get him back on track. He was confident that while he could not save his son, my voice or presence could. He figured if anyone could reach Bryan, after years of being out of my class and Bryan now being an adult, I could pull him off the ledge again. I connected with Bryan, via social media, and gave him words of encouragement and hope. I also provided him with resources and people to contact that could support him when he was ready to seek them out. While me connecting with Bryan, after all those years apart, did not result in him immediately turning his life around, it did show him that my relationship with him extended far beyond my classroom, and he could continue to count on me to support him during the ups and downs of life.

Relationships rooted in respect can make a world of difference with our students. These relationships show our students that when they need someone, we will go to the ends of the world to be there for them. It means a lot and can accomplish a lot. Taking the emphasis off of content and placing them on connections will end in students gaining the content you need them to gain. Not because they are good at a subject or love it, but they love and respect you and know you love and respect them.

One thing I have learned from being raised in the streets is that you look out for those who look out for you. If you have my back, then I will have your back. If you are willing to take one for me, then I will take one for you. In inner-city schools, we are losing our students to the streets and gangs because they enter our buildings feeling as if no one has their back. They do not feel valued, respected, or visible. Sometimes, students will hide the potential and abilities they possess if they feel their teachers do not value or respect them. Genuine relationships can fill a longing to be accepted by something bigger than ourselves. If we do not attempt to fill these voids that we know exist and show students that our love for them is real, other forces in our society will do the job for us.

## Classroom Strategies for Building Solid Relationships with Students

**This is what WE Do**: At the start of each class period, I initiate something that unites us as a class. It signals to my students that we are ready to begin our day. If it is in the morning, we sing a good morning song. If it is the end of the day, we celebrate because we made it to the end of the day. These gestures not only started us off with positive energy, but it is something small that the students looked forward to doing each day.

When I forgot to sing or celebrate, they reminded me that we forgot. Students even took the initiative to take over the good morning song and celebration, so I did not have to worry. If you are looking for a way to set the tone of your classroom, this is something practical to give a shot.

"Good morning. Good morning. Good morning to you. Our day is beginning; there's so much to do. Good morning. Good morning. Good morning to you and you and you and you!"

**Give Them Something to Talk About**: Social media plays a significant role in the lives of most students—so much that they are missing, and sometimes longing for, the physical interaction with other humans. To break the trend of being anti-social, I give my students something that will generate discussion and relationship building. I start the year off using conversation cards and a conversation ball. When students enter the room, the cards are on their desks, and they take turns connecting with their classmates while I do any administrative tasks. When I have completed my tasks, I then circle the room and see what they are discussing. Do not fret if they are talking about something that is not on the card. They are talking. When this happens, I listen to their stories, jump in the conversation, or use this time to impart knowledge or give them something to think about. I also use this time to check on students with the simple question: "you good?" To bring the class back together, I toss a giant beach ball around the room with the same questions from the connection cards on it. Whomever I toss the ball to must select a question and respond to it. I also respond to this question before I toss it to another student. If something else is a trending topic, I have students share the story with me and allow the class time to discuss. They always want to hear my opinion on something. So, I always use this as a way to step into their world and see what is going on.

**Catch 'Em And Reel 'Em In**: I begin each lesson with a personal story or reflection on the topic of the day. I frequently connect the story to my family, life, or a personal struggle with what I am teaching. When this happens, the content becomes personal. I love using images, quotes, or songs to present my thoughts, opinions, or feelings. They take the bait every time. Sometimes we move on to our content in laughter, and other times in tears. However we get there, and when we arrive, they are begging for more. Try to make what you teach personal, even if it tells the story about how you struggled to learn the content to teach it to them. Transparency with your students encourages them to take walls down that hinder relationship building. When they see their teachers and peers putting themselves out there, it makes it easy for them to do the same.

**Stay in The Power Zone:** Once you have started your lesson, stay in the power zone. Use your tone, eyes, and body language to connect with each student. Standing at the front of the room makes us appear stand-offish and can disconnect us from students who cringe at authoritative figures. Even in our classroom, we need to be in the trenches. If you are presenting a lecture, you should be amongst the crowd. When students are engaged in small group activities, you should be interacting with each group and using this opportunity to check for understanding and provide constructive feedback. Being amongst the students presents the perfect opportunity to not only conduct mini-lessons with students, but also a time to pick up vibes and emotions students may have. Our students need to see and know that we are always there and willing to give a hand when needed. Being in close proximity to students not only helps us manage our classrooms, but it also helps us develop solid relationships with our students.

**Constant Conferences**: Make it a point to check-in with students regularly. Do not be so "content-minded that you are no classroom good" and missing out on personal interactions with your students. Our students need us, but many will not let us know. If you sense something is off about a student, deal with it in a personal and respectful manner. Constant conferences with students can help diffuse a situation before it gets out of control, no matter what it may be. If it is during class time, adjust and get the ninety-nine started but go after that one. Studies have shown that students are not just acting out for any reason. Although they may not open up to you immediately, sometimes they just need to be in the presence of peace and someone who genuinely cares. Don't wait until it's too late to notice the signs were there and their flashlights were signaling for help.

**Stop, Drop, and Roll with It**: When something is trending in their lives, communities, or the world, students need adults to help them process what's occurring in a responsible, appropriate, and compassionate manner. While sometimes, they are looking for our opinion and guidance; other times, they just need to let it out and talk about it. Roll with it and, if possible, teach from it. Yeah, we all have content to teach, but your content will fall on absent minds if your students are checked out. Sometimes us just stepping into their world, no matter how long it may take, can help them check back in.

**Be Where It Is Happening:** Anyone who has worked with me will tell you that I love pep rallies, the hallways, and kicking it in the cafeteria. I do not like only to be where my students are, but I love to be where all students are. I find joy in eating lunch with students, meeting students in the hallway, and learning the latest dances at the pep rally. Even when I have to be there, as a part of duty, I love being there. I make the most of it. I use this opportunity to gain respect--not clout. These are the spaces where students can see that we are humans who love to laugh and have a good time. If you have never just "kicked it" with your students, their friends, or students, in general, go for it and be free!

# TWO

# ENGAGING STUDENTS IN A CULTURALLY RELEVANT AND REALISTIC MANNER

---

*"Young Black [dude] trap and he can't change it; know he a genius, he just can't claim it cause they left him no platforms to explain it; he frustrated, so he gets faded but deep down inside he knows you can't fade him."*

NIPSEY HUSSLE, *DEDICATION*, 2019

---

As I wait to turn the corner and pull into the teacher's parking lot, each morning, I count the number of students going in the opposite direction of the school. Even when the first bell of the day is ringing, students are leaving. The idea of skipping school is puzzling to me now, as an educator. However, I am all too familiar with the "why" behind ditching school and skipping classes. In junior high and high school, I actively did both because the school did not meet my needs, so I went seeking fulfillment elsewhere. School is supposed to be a place of self-discovery, excitement, and learning for students.

Most importantly, it is supposed to be a place of refuge. So, what is it about our schools and classrooms, especially those in urban spaces, that push students away and run them off instead of inviting them inward? From my experience and perspective, the answer is simple--our students learn more about themselves, in an engaging and meaningful manner, while in the streets than they do while in our schools and classrooms.

I think I mastered the skill of ditching school and skipping classes from my older brother. Teachers and administrators considered him as a growing menace to society, but in my eyes, he was brilliant. At a young age, he developed a rogue personality and always went against the grain. When given clear instructions on what not to do, he consistently defied them and *always* stayed in trouble. Currently serving out a prison sentence, his journey in and out of the prison system started at a very early age. On the days he did attend school, he was plotting his way to get out and explore the streets. One of the many things I admired about him was that he was a walking dictionary who gleaned over game designs and the engineering behind the music he loved. Place him in a setting that had to do with science, technology, or penning lyrics, and he would thrive. However, those options were not available to underprivileged kids in South Central. During the late 1990s and early 2000s, STEM programs in my hood were unheard of (or my grandmother just couldn't afford to send us to them), so my brother went out to find them on his own. Do not get me wrong; every trip that my brother took beyond the school walls was not for self-discovery. However, I believe that he learned more about himself, his skills, and talents while roaming the streets than he did while in school. To have not formally graduated from elementary, middle school, or high school, my brother is and was a very "smart" man. He is a self-taught man who is currently into psychology and engineering. I imagine where he could be now if the schools made a point to grab hold of him and speak to his emotional, social, and academic needs. Instead, he fell through the cracks of our education system.

He was pushed out of schools (through suspensions and expulsions) right down the pipeline to prison. My question to educators is, why? We must question why students enter schools with potential, but would instead leave and offer all of their gifts and talents to the streets. Why is it that when students are going in the opposite direction of the school, we are not aggressively hunting them down and welcoming them back into our buildings? Lastly, what is out in the streets that is captivating to our students, and what can we take from the streets and apply to our curriculums, classrooms, and schools?

I am convinced that good teaching by good educators could have captured my brother's heart and mind before he became a delinquent. A good educator uses Culturally Relevant and Culturally Responsive pedagogy to "attend to students' academic needs" in order to get them to "choose academic excellence" (Ladson-Billings, 1995). They know that, as Geneva Gay (2018) succinctly contends "every student can do well" even if their "capabilities are not directly translatable to classroom learning, they can still be used by teachers as points of reference and motivational devices to evoke student interest and involvement in academic affairs." With this in mind, good teachers strive to know their students holistically and understand the importance of including students' cultural references in the learning opportunities provided. So, when our students enter their classrooms and schools, they see more of themselves and what they value, instead of what is important to us as educators.

Furthermore, our schools prepare students to be agents of change and "develop students' consciousness about the sociopolitical factors that affect their teaching and learning" (Emdin, 2011). A good educator also strives to incorporate and validate the realities of their students by finding ways to improve their effectiveness by bringing aspects of students' communities and culture into their learning spaces. I believe that Culturally Relevant/Culturally Responsive Pedagogy and Reality Pedagogy should be at the top of every educator's list of effective pedagogical practices to engage all students. Combined, and if properly implemented, these pedagogical practices provide us with the tools necessary to transform the learning experiences of students and has the potential to change the way they view school and learning in general. However, it is prominent that we first get to know our students because "we can't teach what and who we do not know" (Gay, 2018).

## Understand Their Positionality

When we interact with our students, we tend to interact with them at face value. We assess them based on what we see them as on the outside, and the little bits and pieces they share with us to let us know what's on the inside. In education, many of us get it wrong when it comes to determining what our students need in and from our schools. We fail to meet their needs, mainly because we make decisions based on assumptions and our own biases. Most educators look at their students and attempt to address their needs based on their surface-level evaluations. What I mean by this is that they fail to consider the positionality of their students. Referencing the work of Frances A. Maher and Mary Kay Tetreault (1993), considering one's positionality means to consider how "gender, race, class, and other aspects of our identities are markers of relational *positions* rather than essential qualities." What this means for us, as educators, is that in order to meet the needs of our students in the classroom, and help them develop into active participants in our learning environments, we must understand that "the fashioning of one's voice in the classroom is largely constituted by one's position there" (Maher & Tetreault, 118). According to scholars Juanita Johnson-Bailey and Ronald M. Cervero (1998), "the concepts of positionality addresses how the cultures, genders, races, ages, and sexual orientations of teachers and students act and interact in the classroom environment." More than any other factors, our positionalities as educators and students, "dictate the learning and patterns of classroom behavior." Teaching and leading "a culturally and linguistically diverse student body warrants that educators examine their own values and assumptions about working with students who are different" from us (Douglas & Nganga, 59). However, as Ty-ton Douglas and Christine Nganga (2013) point out, "pre-service teachers and school leaders are given far too few opportunities to reflect on, inquire about, and interrogate who they are as human beings, developing pedagogies, and critical agents/facilitators of anti-oppressive 21st-century classrooms and schools." To meet the diverse needs of our students, we must understand our position in relation to our students and how they position themselves in various settings.

Our students are sophisticated individuals whom we must study to get to the root of how our schools can meet their individual needs. But, again, students' positionality is hard to understand because few educators have examined their own and how it shapes their identities or influences what they do, how they navigate inside and outside the classroom, and how they view the students positioned in front of them. Let's be honest, when was the last time you asked yourself how your race, class, gender, ethnicity, and worldview, shape the way you interact with your students or the learning experiences and opportunities you provide for your students? The concept of positionality was something that I was introduced to during my graduate studies. Because my graduate studies focused on Urban Education, we were constantly challenged to evaluate our own positionalities in the context of who we teach, what we teach, and how we teach. However, prior to this degree program, I had never considered how my own positionality, and the factors that influence how I position myself in certain spaces, influenced the decisions I made in my classroom and how I viewed my students. Honestly, because I held a limited view of some of my students, I withheld them from opportunities and resources I felt were above them or too challenging for their intellectual abilities.

So, again, have you reflected on your positionality? Have you reflected on who you are and how these factors shape your interactions with students and the learning opportunities and experiences you provide to students? Are you meeting the social, emotional, cultural, and academic needs of your students through a lens of equity and using their positions to influence your pedagogy and teaching? These questions can be answered through an honest reflection on where you stand in your classrooms and how you view your students from the position in which you are located.

Knowing the positionalities of our students can provide us with the information we need to meet them where they are as learners and build them up to where we want them to be as scholars. Understanding the factors that shape who our students are, in relationship to others, and in the context of school, can also help us understand what keeps students excited about school and learning and what pushes them away from our schools and classrooms. For example, being raised in a non-traditional family structure (which was common in our community) was pivotal in how I viewed the world. In contrast to the nuclear family structure, my grandmother had assumed the role of my mother while my uncles took turns serving as the male presence in our lives. We were raised in a poor, drug/gang-infested part of Los Angeles, but were somewhat middle-class. My grandmother was a homeowner and worked long and hard to keep her home. On many occasions, her sons stepped in to make sure she could make ends meet each month. My grandmother was born in a small town in North Louisiana but moved to Northern California at a young age. She graduated high school and took some classes in college but got married, pregnant, and began her life as a wife and mother at a very young age. She moved to Los Angeles in the 1960s, where she would raise her family. Out of seven children, only a handful of them graduated from high school. My uncle, Benny, was the only one who went on to attend the local community college, where he graduated with an A.A. degree in Communications. My grandmother took education seriously and wanted me to accomplish more than what she could as a black woman growing up in northern California. However, she did not know where to start to ensure that my siblings and I were successful. Attending school was mandatory, but excelling in school was not encouraged. All she mandated was that we got passing grades and got out of school with a diploma that had our name on it.

Black Christian values dictated our household, but we only attended church on holidays. We were raised to question the intentions of every racial group of people. Liberalism was evident in my home, yet my guardians never claimed a political party. Everything happening around us was a conspiracy, and to be successful in life, all I needed was the primary "three R's"--reading, writing, and arithmetic.

My mother abandoned three kids for drugs, and when she did come around, it was to steal our food stamps or my grandmother's clothes, not to parent. I was a thinker and extraordinarily creative but never really had space or support to do much of that inside my home. Everyone was on the move and trying to stay afloat, so individualized attention from adults was something I was missing. I looked up to my sister and dreamed of the day that I would be a softball player like her until she began drinking, stripping, and snorting cocaine. I did not want to go that route.

I was a cheerleader and a competitive bowler, which helped keep me off the streets (bowling did help pay for college, too). However, I participated in these activities to fulfill my desire to be social. I loved to talk! Talking always got me in trouble in class and was the reason behind me continually being told to leave. I frequently slept in class but mainly on the days after my siblings and I went on a hunt searching for our mom. Our grandmother did the best she could to raise us. She gave us what she could, but it did not fill the voids we had. Her efforts, also, did not stop us from scouring local crack houses and apartments looking for our mother. The relationship between my mother and father was violent because they were both addicts. I do not remember much about them being together, but I was often told and reminded about the abuse she suffered at his hands.

Gang violence was prevalent on my block. We mastered the skill of questioning any car driving slowly down the street and how to duck and dodge bullets well in our adolescence. We played outside, but that was at our own risk because a shooting could happen at any moment. We did it, however, because family surrounded us. Since most of our friends were raised by an extended family member or our parents got high together, we felt like we understood each other when no one else did. That is my positionality.

When I entered schools, my positionality shaped who I would let in, how I interacted with others, and what I sought to get out. Because I was looking for attention, I loved to be the center of attention in the classroom, so I became the class clown. I did not trust my mother, so I either found fault in any female authority figure or sought to make her the mother I never had. In the classroom, this translated in me often being in conflict with my female teachers. I was loyal to my uncle and grandmother because they were loyal to me. I was driven to please them but also desired encouragement beyond mediocrity. Because of my respect for them, if a teacher involved them in educational decisions, I generally responded well. I loved to talk but did not have permission to express myself, so I was defiant and talked in class anyway, especially when collaboration with peers was not allowed. I did not receive any consequences at home, so I was not scared of the consequences at school. I wanted "more," materialistic things, to be like some of my peers, so I stole it from local stores in the mall, and when my guardians were too busy to remind me to bathe or go to bed, I slept in class or did not go to school at all because school was boring, it did not meet the various social, emotional, or cultural needs that I had, and expectations for me to excel were pretty low.

I ditched school because no one noticed or cared enough to ask about where I was going. I can recall the numerous times my homegirls and I would hop the fence or walk straight out the front gate, and no administrator or teacher even noticed. While roaming the streets, I was able to go to places that I was cautioned not to and learned a lot on the way. All of my hurt, trauma, and pain I packed into a bag, took it to school with me and unpacked it on anyone who crossed a line I had drawn. I stood in the middle of absentee parents, drugs and gang violence, low expectations, and looking for acceptance. I regularly turned from one section to the other, trying to make sense of my world and where I felt I belonged. I was on a quest to learn what teachers were not teaching me as well as where I belonged.

Understanding the positionality of ourselves and our students cannot be emphasized enough because it dictates how we view ourselves, how we view others, or what we assume about ourselves or others. Understanding positionality can also help us, as educators, understand the power that we have, especially regarding the decisions we make in our learning spaces and the opportunities we provide to our students. Positionality allows us to understand how our students view themselves and the world. But it also provides educators with the insight necessary to design curriculum and learning experiences that provide access to learning and reinforce, affirm, validate students' cultures, identities, experiences, and worldviews. This knowledge is like gold when building our cultural competencies, as conscious educators, and school curriculums and culture. Knowing how students position themselves, or the socio-political factors that influence their positionality, can help us ensure that we meet the social, emotional, cultural, and academic needs of the diverse student populations that exist in inner-city schools.

Working in the service industry, we cannot adequately serve if we do not know our market or clientele. Understanding one's positionality goes beyond a Q&A session. Understanding students' positionality requires us to dig deep and be innovative. Educators must allow students the opportunity to show us what is important to them. This information is necessary if we plan to prepare students to reflectively and effectively address the social ills in their worlds. If you have yet to examine your positionality, I encourage you to do so before you move onto the next section. It will give you a new perspective.

## Allow Students to Take Risk on Path of Self Discovery

"Be home when the streetlights come on" was the primary rule that governed my siblings and me when we were playing outside. Despite the violence, drugs, and gangs that surrounded us, we loved our hood, and we knew the inside and out of the Rolling 100s. Until the sun began to set, we had all afternoon and evening to explore our "hood," and that we did. Whether this was on foot or piling up on each other's bikes, we hit the streets daily, looking for an adventure. Each year, as we got older, the experiences got grander. We started by exploring local parts of the neighborhoods, such as stealing loquats off the neighbor's tree and making a neighbor's pool house our clubhouse at night. Our journeys escalated to sneaking on the bus and riding to wherever our desires led us for the day. Despite all the chaos and confusion of my childhood, my days of adventure are something I would never forget. I got to see my community for what it was and discovered parts of Los Angeles that I never knew existed. This freedom to roam is what introduced me to a whole new world and piqued my desire to want more in life. What I saw on television stepped out of the box and made me chase after my dreams, whatever the cost. I lost interest in school because I had a world to see, and my teachers refused to show it to me. So, I went out to explore it on my own.

My late uncle Benny always said that educators must be mindful of the time we have with our students. We only have them for eight hours of the day, while society has them for the remaining 16 hours. Each minute they spend with us should be intentional because students have greater forces to combat when they leave our schools. If you drive through many of your inner-city neighborhoods, after school hours, you will witness kids of all ages outside playing discovery. The opportunities for paid adventures and vacations are usually limited, so, especially during summer and winter breaks, they make their adventures. One of the many unique things about students in urban communities is their conditions and environments have shaped them into innovative risk-takers who can make something out of nothing. Many educators do not see this potential in the classroom. What they see is a child who can't sit still or keep quiet but fail to realize that exploring, strategizing, and socializing are the norm for them. To effectively serve students in urban communities, we must teach the way they learn. Classrooms in urban schools must provide students with learning experiences that will allow them to do what they know how to do best, go out there and get it.

I have always been complimented on my ingenuity, creativity, and drive. I am not this way because I want to be, but because I had to be growing up poor, black, and female. By the time I was in high school, I had mastered the skill of "making something out of nothing," and that was well before I had access to the internet. When outside playing, we had to come up with creative ways to stay away from gang violence and drug transactions. If we wanted to go outside of the neighborhood, we had to devise a plan of getting to our destination and making it back home before anyone knew we were gone. This planning required a lot of effort and collaboration in the age of no cell phones or social media. We were taking a risk ditching school or sneaking out of the neighborhood.

However, I have learned more from the self-exploration and risks than I learned from my primary and secondary schooling. When I did make it to college, my drive, curiosity, and hustler spirit are what prepared me.

A disconnect between educators and students is created by this prevailing belief that we must dictate what, when, and how they will learn. However, this goes against the upbringing of many kids in urban communities. I did not have someone always around guiding me along the way. I was told what to do around our home and knew that I had to have it completed by the time my grandmother made it home. If I had a project that had to be completed at school and did not have the supplies that were needed, we did not run to the store to purchase supplies. Instead, I was sent around the house to find what was useful. I often turned in projects that were bonded together with glue made out of the water, salt, and flour we had at home. We had to use what we had to get what we wanted.

In our schools exist some of the most innovative, talented, and entrepreneurial spirits. Many students from urban communities would be Google's dream employee. However, because we are not giving them the space to show their ingenuity, they go elsewhere. They possess the 21st Century Skills that we promote; it is just packed in a different way and coded in a language that some educators are not interested in under-standing. Bringing this potential out of them is going to take constant creativity and innovation on our end. We want to see our students explore their options and take risks, but we are afraid to do so ourselves.

## Be A Community Classroom

I loved my neighborhood growing up. Despite being filled with drugs and crime, I loved my block and community. Especially after the release of the movie *Friday* in 1995, I was proud to say I lived "'round here...between Normandie and Western." What I loved so much about my community was the fact that the people of my community understood me. We understood one another. We loved one another. And, most importantly, we had each other's back. No matter what the need was, we

stuck together. The bonds that we had extended far back to the relationships that our parents had and that their parents had. Despite going our
separate ways--some in jail, off to college, or to another city or state--
when we go back into the community, we are welcomed with open arms.
I knew that members of my community, despite their struggles, always
wanted what was best for me. I could count on them to keep an eye on
me to ensure that I did not get off-track. For those who were going in the
wrong direction, they were swooped up quickly by the "big homies" to
make sure they did not become outsiders in their community. Growing
up in South Central was a struggle, but one that created big visions.
These visions placed you back in that same community rebuilding it,
creating jobs, or reforming the education system. Every person from my
neighborhood had one thing in common. We wanted to change it but did
not know how or where to start.

When I went to school, most teachers did not know the community
where I lived. They thought they knew it but had no idea. They came to
the local schools to teach. However, when they finished with their work-
day, they went back to the comfort of their lives off in some suburban or
up and coming area of Los Angeles. Many would often remark how they
would not be "caught dead in this area after dark," forgetting that we had
to live in "this area" after dark. They made degrading comments about
the area, never stopping to consider how those from the city would feel. I
often questioned how an educator could want what was best for me if
they did not see any potential in my community. They did not see potential because their view was one that was limited to what made the local
news or the rumors that were spoken throughout the teacher's lounge. I
always dreaded the day that I would run into my teachers in the store,
but those days were few in numbers. The ones who I did run into were
of an older generation and had been well established in the community
before it "turned sour." To me, it was essential to see the faces of influence
from my school in my community. Seeing my teachers made me feel like
they saw real potential in me because they saw potential in my neighborhood. They saw past the drug dealing and gang violence and knew that
there was more to the community than what their eyes could see. The

stock they held in the city ensured that the products coming out of the community were of quality. With this in mind, they took time to help construct each piece of product with love and care. They saw the social ills of the community. But, instead of allowing that to push them away, they drew in closer. They took their craft more seriously and sought to educate and equip a generation who could return to their communities and serve as game-changers.

Educators who work in community schools must have ties and investments to the community. If you live in the neighborhood or not, your presence is essential. How can we teach kids from the community if we know nothing about it or what we do know is rooted in assumptions, stereotypes, or a cultural deficit? Educators should be out in the community, getting to know what the area is about, what is vital to the people, and how we can support their vision in our schools.

The one thing that has continued to sadden me in this profession is to see educators working with a student and have no genuine interest in that student as a whole being. I recall one time sitting in a meeting and us discussing the construction of apartment complexes around the school. The principal announced that most of the newly constructed buildings would serve as affordable housing for Section 8 recipients. Many of my colleagues gasped, and one went so far to comment, "and we know those students will be the cream of the crop" in the most condescending and demeaning tone. It hurts to know that an educator would make such a remark about the potential of a student based on their housing status. How could that educator effectively serve if they already had a preconceived notion of a student based on the stereotypes associated with their living conditions?

Our students want to know that their communities matter to us. In the same manner that they want to see themselves reflected in our learning spaces, they want to see their communities reflected in our learning spaces. It is possible to bring communities into the classroom, but first, we must take time out to go out into them. With any content area, the communities that we teach can be brought into our classrooms to enhance instruction. However, this cannot be the community that we think we know but the community for what it is and all the beauty it has to offer.

One thing I find joy in doing is eating at local restaurants or shopping at the local grocery stores after work. On the weekend, I would bring my kids to the local parks, attend events hosted at the local recreational center, or see a play at the local theater. I attend as many school events as possible to be in the presence of community members. One thing I love is accepting students' invites to Sunday morning service or a family/community gathering.

When we spend our money in the communities where our students live, we are helping these communities thrive. When we spend time in their communities outside the comfort of the school, we get to see the community through a different lens. Seeing our students, their families, and their community through a new lens allows us to understand the cultural assets that they bring to our school community. We also see the social capital that we can gain from their presence in our schools. In our classrooms, we must use their assets to enhance our learning environments and use their community as a foundation for our teaching. In a community classroom, the educator values the community. They respect the community. And, they use the beauty of the community to carefully design lessons and learning opportunities that esteem the community and prepare students to transform any social ills or inequities in their communities.

## Get Your "Hussle" On

On March 31, 2019, rapper Ermias "Nipsey Hussle" Asghedom was murdered outside of his Los Angeles clothing store--Marathon Clothing. Here we are, one year later, "safe at home" and, some, remembering the life and legacy of "Neighborhood Nip." When the news broke of Nipsey Hussle's killing, not only did the hip-hop community feel a blow to the gut, but urban spaces throughout the United States, and kids in these spaces, felt it as well. Me--a girl from South Central--also felt this blow.

Nipsey Hussle was more than an ex-gang member who turned into a successful gangsta rapper. A product of the same South Central streets he walked and died on, to me, he was a prime example of the type of student educators should seek to create. However, we often overlook them in our classrooms.

My younger brothers introduced me to Nipsey Hussle a few years ago on a ride home from the airport. His desire to redevelop South Central, talks about financial freedom, and his empowering of the South Central hip-hop culture connected us to him immediately. He was one of "us," and, most importantly, he wanted better for "us." Where I come from, when you make it out, you stay out. But, up until the time of his death, Nipsey Hussle was proof that you could make it out of South Central and come back. His goal was to reinvest and "double-up" South Central, Los Angeles by making it better or more profitable than before. The streets that others would consider the "mud," Nipsey saw gold and treated them as such.

Nipsey was both streets smart and book smart, which made him great. These qualities also made him a role model for many young kids, from South Central, who saw no way out of their current conditions. But, like many students growing up in urban communities, his greatness was overlooked in the classroom. He often spoke in interviews about being "gifted and talented," but no one knew his status because his schools refused to test him. When they finally did, he was identified as gifted and talented but had already given up on school altogether.

Listening to Nipsey Hussle's 2018 Grammy-nominated album, *Victory Lap*, I wonder what else he could have accomplished in his lifetime if educators tapped into his genius before he had dropped out of school. Nipsey was a self-taught and innovative game-changer. His street knowledge took him from successfully selling $100 CDs out of his trunk to topping the Billboard charts. The passion he had for his community, and interest in math, science, and technology, motivated him to redevelop his neighborhood. In doing so, he created jobs and opened up schools and community/business centers devoted to STEM and youth programs.

All of the greatness that flowed through the DNA of Nipsey Hussle walked through school buildings often overlooked. His peers noticed his greatness, but the educators he encountered did not. At least not enough to stop him before the streets got to him. He knew he was a genius, but he could not claim it. In his schools, they left him no platform to explain it. So, before he could graduate from high school, he dropped out. The Rolling 60 Crips, and making money selling weed, had captured his heart. Despite his success, his trajectory can be seen as a failure by educators to grab hold of him, in a meaningful way, and help him understand his true potential in the context of education.

We have Nipsey Hussles walking all through our schools feeling trapped in an education system that is failing them. But this ends today! It is time for educators to reevaluate our perceptions, and the misconceptions, of a "gifted" student. Just because a student does not fit into our narrow, standard, and, if I'm honest, the Eurocentric mold of an acceptable student does not mean they are not deserving of our real and unfailing love. Just because their cultural customs and norms do not align with ours does not make them undeserving of quality education. Only because they express themselves in a manner that some of us would never understand, that does not permit us to discredit all the exceptional qualities and abilities that they possess. Just because they come from communities that might make some of us uncomfortable, that does not excuse us from checking our biases and privileges that might hinder them from obtaining access to an equitable education. Just because their gifts and talents are packaged in a manner that is different from what we are used to, does not mean they do not exist. Sometimes, we have to step out of our norms and comfort, connect with students, and make an effort to see what lies beneath the surface. Sometimes, this might require us to hustle harder than we've had to do for other students and change the way we teach just for that student.

So, as you think about your students, which many of us are during these uncertain times, think about those students who you see but overlook. Who is your Nipsey Hussle? What are their passions and gifts? How can we use their positionality to address their social, cultural, and community needs in our classrooms and schools? How can we use their cultural capital to design a curriculum that is responsive to their cultural needs and enriched with opportunities to evaluate their current realities? How can we use their street smarts to push them to greater heights? How can we double up and change the game in our classes and inspire them to do so in their hoods? How can we transform the way we do teaching and learning to transform the way they view school? You know the Neighborhood Nips in your schools. Last time I checked, they were the ones who were dedicated to hustling and motivating others even when some counted them out. They've been grinding all of their lives because they believed--when no one else did--that they could go higher in life. So, go get 'em! Every student who reminds you of Nipsey Hussle, I challenge you to make them your ONE. Bring them into your space and show them the possibilities. Go get your "hussle on" because every student deserves an educator who is willing to take a victory lap with them.

## Classroom Strategies for Engaging Students in a Culturally Relevant and Realistic Manner

**What's on Your Playlist?** Music can tell us a lot about our students. Have you taken a moment to ask what they are listening to and listen to it? If not, a great strategy to use, to connect with, and get to know your students is a class playlist. Every six weeks, I would have my students write down their favorite songs at the current moment in their lives (the clean version). I would then use their songs to develop a playlist in Apple Music for each class period. While students were working, we would listen to the playlist as a class. When it was time to share out, if your song came on, it was your time to take the stage. The students loved hearing their favorite songs during class, and some could not wait until the new marking period to change their tunes. Many of the songs became my favorite, and I learned a lot about my students. I learned who my activists, dreamers, dancers, rappers, singers, and overall musicians were. I learned those who were experiencing joy and also about those who were experiencing pain. I even learned, from a popular song at the time, that suicidal thought was a trend among my students and man, that was very eye-opening. Not only does a playlist give you and your students something to jam to (if a dance party happens, roll with it), the songs also start great conversations. Allow students to share their song selection and what makes them connect with it, if you want to get to know your students!

**Better Together**: Kids in urban spaces are accustomed to socialization and collaboration. In our classrooms, it is beneficial for students to work together. Students thrive off of interaction and communication. In our classes, this should be happening all the time. Almost every assignment that I give, I allow students to work with a partner or with a group. Yes, even on classroom assessments, they can work in groups. I believe this is the best way to get them to discuss content and demonstrate their under-standing of the material. It is also a great way to check for understanding and provide on the spot mini-lessons. To students, showing what they know and can do to their peers is also a great confidence booster, and that's what it's all about, building them up! I love hearing them bounce ideas off of each other and problem-solving together. Allowing students to collaborate with their peers, in a familiar setting, also helps them exchange social capital and incorporates the 21st-century skills of collab-oration and communication into any lesson.

**Community Maps**: Community mapping is a great way to get to know the communities our students come from and what is important to them and their communities. Community maps are not limited to content areas and can be used to explore content in various disciplines. It is also a way to teach students about ourselves, each other, and how cultural values can differ according to communities. In this activity, students who live in the same communities work together to create a visual sketch of their community. If there is someone in the class new to the area or not from the same neighborhood, I place them in a group. In this group, I challenge students to create two communities to compare and contrast.

After they create a visual outline of their communities, they identify major community hubs (recreation centers, parks, churches, schools, barbershops/hair salons, etc.). To extend the activity, they explain what happens in the major hubs and how it contributes to their culture and who they are as an individual. Community maps are a great way to get to understand a student's assumed positionality as well as the social ills in the community and what problems they would address if they could do so. Community maps are empowering to students because it shows that others take an interest in truly learning about where they come from and what makes them great. They are also an effective strategy when creating a sense of community in our classrooms by giving students a hands-on, meaningful, and appropriate way to learn about each other. Leave the maps up throughout the year, and they will serve as talking pieces. Students can use the maps to share things happening in their communities and how their lives are affected by it (positively or negatively) when they enter our schools.

**It Can All Be Fun & Games:** Have you ever had downtime after a lesson and looked to see what your students were doing? I have, and on countless occasions, many of them were playing some type of game! I remember one year in particular when I could not stop my kids from playing Words with Friends, Trivia Crack, and Pool with Friends. Now, it's Clash of Clans or Fortnite. It never fails to look around in a staff meeting and see our colleagues playing games. Games should not only be used to review content but should be a part of everyday life in our classrooms. Through gamification, we can pre-assess, introduce, and teach new content, and check for understanding. Games provide students with a way to strategize and solve solutions. Critical thinking is our end goal, and there are various games out there, old and new, that provide ways to gamify your classes. Games are also a way to promote healthy competition as well as team bonding and building. Don't allow the lie of "it can't always be fun and games" fool you. If playing games is what it takes to teach skills and content simultaneously, then break out the Jenga, blast a Gimkit, or get your musical chairs on. Whatever you do, have fun!

**Student-Designed Choice Boards**: There is no one way to solve a problem or demonstrate mastery of a skill or content. So, when it comes down to student voice in the classroom, why do teachers make it our duty to dictate how a student demonstrates learning and understanding? Shouldn't that be the student's role in the school? Student-designed choice boards are a great way to empower students by giving them a voice and freedom of choice. At the beginning of each unit, provide students with the unit objectives and what they must know and be able to do after the unit. From there, students can collaborate to develop various methods (try to limit to five) they can use to demonstrate learning and a class rubric for evaluation. It would not also hurt to ask students what strategies you should use to teach them the content. Through choice boards, students take ownership of their learning and what they create. Your role is to facilitate the learning process and support them. If they fail, pick them up, dust them off, and encourage them to try again. Students will amaze you with their creations once you remove the rigid instructions and intimidating exemplars. We want to develop students who can thrive in today's world. To accomplish this goal, we must create a space where they can show us what they can do without telling them what to do.

# THREE

# AUTHENTICITY IN MY INTERACTION WITH STUDENTS

---

*"Authenticity is a collection of choices that we have to make every day. It's about the choice to show up and be real. The choice to be honest. The choice to let our true selves be seen."*

BRENÉ BROWN

---

Entering high school was my chance at a fresh start. I was a well-known troublemaker in middle school, and I had a last name--Toomes--that was synonymous with "up to no good." Before high school, I begged my grandmother and my uncle to allow me to attend a school where no one knew me or anyone in my family (especially my brother). My brother's shadow had become my own, and I was tired of living in it. I desperately needed and wanted a fresh start. Beginning the ninth grade at a school where not too many people knew me or knew the "mess" that was my life was a big deal for me. I made a promise to keep my hands clean, per se, and I needed an environment that was going to help me stay on the right track.

A new high school allowed me to hide my mess and create a new identity that no one had known or had seen before. However, that became a
more difficult task than just being the true me. Not only was I lying
about my address to attend school in a different district (that presented
better opportunities), I lied about everything else that made up me. I
created these bizarre stories about the neighborhood I was from, the
"state-funded vacation" my mom was on, and why my grandmother and
uncle were raising me. The secrets that slowly slipped out in middle
school, I got to tuck back in and cover-up. However, when all the mess I
tried to hide reached its capacity, my walls came tumbling down, and I
was not able to keep it together on my own.

I laugh when I look back at my high school days and how much effort I
put into being everything I thought my family was not. My efforts were
in vain because it was only so long that I could hide the true me. I was a
cheerleader, on the step team, member of the Black History Club, and
even a Lion's Club Speech Contest winner. But none of that was me. I
was a skater girl, a "prep," and anything else that was opposite of my
gang-affiliated family. Still, I was not me. No uniform, fancy clothes, or
edited speeches could help fill the voids I had, so, again, I went searching
for the people and things that could make me feel whole. Seeking what
could make me whole took me on an adventure. This adventure is the
same one that we witness many students journey on as they try to figure
out when and where they can enter and who is real enough to help them
discover their true selves. I just wanted to know that someone cared
about me, and this is true for our students as well. However, to have any
impact on the achievement of our students, our actions must speak
louder than our words (Gay, 2018).

## Take Your Game Face Off

When I first started my teaching career, I remember hearing the classic
instructions of "don't smile before Christmas." Later, I came to find out
that all new educators hear this little piece of bad advice. If we wanted to
be taken seriously by our students, we had to look "serious." Sadly, many

educators become so accustomed to looking serious that the resting prick face has become their routine and daily look. Some educators feel this image makes them effective in the classroom and helps them manage their classes with an "iron fist." However, it is working against them and pushing them further away from their students. If negative words can trigger anxiety in the brain, imagine what tense facial expressions and body language do to the minds of our students.

The face that we wear daily says a lot to our students. It communicates to them how we feel about them and how we feel about our jobs. If your face says loud and clear that you despise what you are doing (at least until Christmas), then it sends a message that you dislike the students that you should be serving. If we want to be realistic, every day is not a happy day for us--teachers are human too. However, I think it is better to allow our students to see us as adults who process real emotions. We have to model healthy ways of dealing with those emotions without taking it out on others. The faces that we wear are essential to our students because it is our first line of communication with them. When students are trying to feel our vibe, the first thing they look at is our face, and from there, they make an initial assessment of if we are indeed an authentic person or not.

We all have the "game face" that we wear when we are ready to get down to business. However, your face should welcome students to an exciting game, not one that is intimidating and impersonal. Take a moment to think back to that teacher who made a difference in your life. Your initial liking and connection with them probably had nothing to do with the content that they taught, but the face that they chose to wear. I say "chose to wear" because the difference between smiling and frowning is a simple choice. Despite the trials that we face in our personal or professional lives, we must make a choice to get up every morning and put on our smiles.

That educator who influenced you first had to inspire you. To inspire you, they had to make a conscious decision, daily, that despite what was happening in their lives, they were going to smile. Their smiles were going to radiate in the room and excite those who were in it. From that smile, empowerment came, and whatever the task was for the day, their smile communicated to you that everything was going to be alright. When students enter our spaces, we must be mindful that some of them may feel as if there is no reason to smile. The burdens that they carry are so heavy that it has crippled their ability to find joy, especially in schools. The last thing students need is to encounter adults who also struggle with finding joy, and contaminate the learning environments with their gloomy countenance.

To this day, I still remember the face of my high school math teacher Ms. Hyde—from her light-skinned complexion that adorned with freckles down to her pearly white teeth that complemented her hair as it hung down to her face. Every day, she greeted us at the door with her excitement and her smile. Her smile set the tone for the room. In a way, it was her classroom management. Now, don't get me wrong; she did get frustrated at times, but she followed her frustration with a smile. Seeing her smile made it feel as if the California sun was shining a little bit brighter in her room. The game face she chose to wear daily was one that pushed me to learn math and supported me when I struggled. Her game face moved me to enroll in any class she was teaching. The sight of her smile calmed my anxieties about math and many other issues I carried to school with me. Ms. Hyde was consistent in who she was and the faces that she wore daily. To myself and many of my peers, that's what made her likable, relatable, and real. She held no punches when it came down to getting the job done and teaching math, but no matter how hard she pushed and pricked, we knew it was from a place of love because her face told us so. She smiled before, during, and after Christmas and created a learning environment that was structured yet fun. Math was happening in Ms. Hyde's room, and everyone wanted to be there. She got us in the game, and how she wore her "game face" inspired us to play the game, and we did it well if I do say so myself. It's okay to smile. It's inspirational to smile.

## You Ain't Gotta Lie to Kick It

One quality that every person values from those who are in their inner circle are people who are true to themselves and true to others. Throughout my teenage years, what I clung to most was those whose words matched their actions--those I knew that I could trust without a shadow of a doubt. In my life, there have only been a few people who I was confident that I could depend on, and I remained loyal and faithful to them. At a very early age, I developed a strong distrust for my mother and father, and to be honest, I still struggle when it comes to trusting them until this day. What caused this mistrust was numerous unfulfilled promises. Because I did not believe my parents to match their words with their actions, I was wary of others who came with words of gold (although I frequently fell in with the wrong crowd of people because they talked a good talk).

At the start of every school year, I met teacher after teacher who talked a good game but did not back it up with their actions. If I did not trust my parents, why would I trust *them*? They promised to treat me with respect, love, and encourage me and push me until I have accomplished all that was in my potential. However, all of that fancy talk went away by the sixth week of school. When they started to experience all the baggage I was carrying around with me, they gave up, and so I gave up as well.

I knew for sure that when I could not trust the words of adults, I had friends that I could trust, and since they had proven their loyalty to me, I had shown my dedication to them. Whatever they needed or wanted, I was down for it. They had my back, and so I had theirs. Even when they requested for me to do something that I knew was wrong, I went along for the ride. I did foolish things because I desperately yearned for loyalty because I was missing this from the two people I desired to receive it from the most.

"I don't trust anybody," is a common phrase that came out of my mouth and one that I continuously hear from my students. Our parents disrupted my ability to trust with their failed actions and broken promises. If my dad said he was going to pick me up at 6:00 pm but never showed, how can I trust someone else to show up when they say they will? If my mother said she was taking our monthly ration of food stamps to the store to buy food yet instead sold them for drugs and left her children hungry, how can I trust you to keep true to your words of feeding into my life and not taking things away from me?

Just like our face and body language are vital in our interactions with students, so are the words we speak and our loyalty to those words. Sadly, I have witnessed many students develop a sour taste for school because of the educators who spoke words and made promises to students that they failed to keep. To them, it was no big deal, but to that student, it was yet again another person saying one thing and doing another.

I am also cautious of my "first day of school self," because sometimes that is where the lies and false realities--rather intentional or unintentional--begin. We are seeking the acceptance of our students just as much as they are trying to gain our approval. We give students a grand vision of what we desire our school year to be like, how our classroom will function, and how we will make personal connections with every student. Our students hold on to every word we speak and become excited at the dream we have sold them. Then, when the school year gets in full swing, every word uttered, and fantasy sold flies out the window--and sadly, students' trust in us is lost. Urban spaces are full of educators who "lied to kick it." They say one thing to win the influence of the community or a household and then do another behind their back. Unfortunately, in many urban communities, there are also family dynamics developed and broken by people who have "lied, to kick it." And, sadly, many schools in urban communities employ adults who lie to kick it. Students in these schools sense it, and instead of having yet another adult in their face lying, they would instead go and risk finding something or someone that will keep it real with them. Be wary of using disingenuous words and actions to connect with students because even the slightest deviation can push them away from the connections we desire to have with them.

We have to be mindful of our words and ensure that our words can and will match our actions. If we tell our students that we are going to do something, then we have a responsibility to see to it that we complete the job, no matter what it takes. In our building, our words and actions should give students hope. We should not become another broken promise or disappointment in their lives. We have all experienced disappointment before, and we remember how that felt. Be mindful of that feeling when interacting with students. They need to see it before they can believe it. Being authentic with students starts with our words. Let our words be our bonds.

## "Ms., She Fake": Is Your Classroom Self Your Hallway Self?

Jemia had the brightest smile and biggest heart. She valued loyalty, honesty, and respect, and she looked for those qualities in her teachers. She did not have the best relationship with her mother, so she especially looked to connect with her female teachers who could serve as role models. She desired them to be the positive maternal figure in her life. She admired ambitious female teachers. Once she felt like she could connect with them, her teachers could count on her to show up, show out, and have your back. However, she expected the same thing from her teachers. Now, Jemia was not naive in who she trusted and opened up to because she had learned the skill of observing and identifying "fake" people. In our school building, she could tell you every teacher who was one person behind closed doors--in their speech and mannerisms--and another person when they were out in the halls interacting with their colleagues or other students.

As educators, we wear many hats and many masks, and yes, we might interact with students and our colleagues on different levels and according to different needs. But there is a stark difference between wearing different hats or code-switching and being fake. It was easy for me to connect with Jemia because I understood why she despised those who were "fake" and valued and respected those who kept it real. See, when someone is "fake," they cannot be trusted because what they are showing you is not who they are. Our students do not show up to our schools and classrooms looking for who we think they should be to them, but they come looking for real and genuine people who they can connect with no matter where.

What I see prevalent in many classrooms are teachers who are trying to be "down." In their words and interactions with students, they are mostly "lying to kick it." They put on a good show in front of students, but when students turn their backs, these teachers morph into a different person. Morphing is also when teachers and administrators show one face to students in public--the good look-- but when they are behind closed doors, the mask and smiles vanish.

What does being "fake," and having a hallway-self and classroom-self have to do with showing students real love? EVERYTHING! Because no one likes a fake person and will try to avoid them at every cost. The ulti-mate form of betrayal is a person who shows you one thing in your one-on-one interactions but becomes another thing when it is no longer just you two. If we feel like this as adults, imagine how our students feel when a "fake" person is their teacher. Students like Jemia come to school looking for people who are going to be real and honest with them in a way that communicates love and respect for them and human beings. They are not asking you to be something that you are not to connect with them; they are just asking you to be you at all times. Students are asking to get a glimpse of your world and the opportunity to see life and experi-ence lessons through your eyes. They want to see your heart, not all the stuff that you use to cover-up what's inside of you. They want to see you be you at all times. They want a person who they know they can come to--with the good and the bad-- and that person can be trusted to give sound advice and keep secrets when in their best interests. They want a person who is not going to be their friend--or enemy--but someone who they can trust to make sound decisions and always operate with their well-being in mind. They want you to show that your concern for them reaches far beyond their academic success and what they can do for you in the classroom. They want and need to know who you show up being is who you are. They need you to be authentically YOU, flaws and all.

## Classroom Strategies to Promote Authenticity

**Multicultural Resources:** One of the most effective ways of promoting authenticity in our classroom is by incorporating multicultural stories, voices, and resources into our content and curriculum. Being an authentic educator means that you care about your students and desire for them to leave your classrooms feeling validated. This can only be accomplished through the usage of a multicultural curriculum and the promotion of a multicultural mindset that fosters empathy while challenging dominant narratives. When selecting material, it is important to assess the historical and cultural accuracy and authenticity of any resources before introducing them to students, and this step should not be overlooked. Authenticity in the classrooms is not just about educators being real. It's also showing your students that their histories, stories, cultures, and communities are real, and you value and respect them.

**What's in Your DNA?** Our DNA tells us everything we need to know about US and others. In this activity, students and teachers can learn about each other by doing DNA analysis. There is no need to go out and purchase an AncestryDNA kit because all you will need is some butcher paper and markers (or even just an outline of a body). Students will create a shape of their body and use this outline to identify what characteristics run through their DNA (Loyalty, Courage, Pride, etc.) As well, they will use this body to explain how they see the world and how they view others. The following features of their body will represent:

Hair: What are their long and short term goals?

Eyes: Issues their eyes witness that they seek to change

Ears: Words of inspiration that can empower others

Mouth: What is their battle cry?

Arms/Hands: How will they use their hands to bring about change in their communities, nations, and world?

Clothing: How does what they wear represent who they are?

Feet: Where have they been, and where are they going?

This activity is excellent for students and teachers alike. Not only does it provide the opportunity to conduct some self-exploration, but it also offers the chance to introduce others to the real and true YOU.

**Drop A Photo**: We have all encountered this on Facebook. You know, those challenges to drop the tenth photo in your phone without making any edits or modifications to them. While this challenge often causes me anxiety, it is an excellent way for friends in the social media world to get a glimpse into our world. This strategy is unique in the classroom (using appropriate images) because it gives us an unfiltered look into the world of our students and vice versa. Periodically, challenge your student to do a photo drop using Google Slides, Jamboard, or Padlet. Select a random number, and have students "drop" a photo, tweet, or post they made. From there, allow students to share in small groups or to the class what was happening when they took the photo or made that particular post. When implementing this strategy, make sure that you are also participating. This activity is more about you than it is about the students. If the goal is to show students our authentic selves, then don't be shy, drop a photo.

**Two-Faced**: We need to understand the masks that our students wear and why they wear those masks. Not only does it provide us a different look into our students, but it also a way for us to introduce our students to our multifaceted faces and the faces of those we encountered. We can tell them that "there are two sides to every coin," but to them, what does that mean? In this activity, students will explore this saying by designing a coin of their own. If they had the opportunity to present their true selves on coinage, what images, symbols, or features would they include on the front of the coin? What about them would be included on the back of the coin? If the currency were to be flipped, which side would be most preferred? The head or the tail? You can also use this activity to explore perspectives or the dynamics of different characters or figures. If a student had to design a coin to represent someone (or something) related to a content area and use their currency to break down a character or concept, what would their medal include to show that everyone and everything is not as simple as it seems?

**Social Media Calendar**: If our students are using social media (Facebook, Twitter, Snap Chat, etc.) to connect with others, then why are we not using social media to communicate with them? Since we are seeking to develop authentic relationships with students, a social media calendar is a great way to help break down any barriers that might exist as well as get students and teachers to open up to each other. A social media calendar, planned by students and teachers, allows for the establishment of days for certain chats to occur and topics that will be discussed. Instead of students interacting with you, while you engage in discourse with your followers, the conversations you are having are directly related to them and their needs. The topics can be serious or humorous, but it should be something the teachers and students agree on and are comfortable with sharing. When developing a social media calendar, or #class-chat, it is best to start small and branch out. Pick one topic for each month and then try to grow the frequency of the chats. Secondly, guide students in picking topics that are inclusive and relevant to all students. I would suggest starting with something light and fun before jumping into anything serious. Lastly, but most importantly, make sure you have instructed your students on digital literacy, citizenship, and the dos and don'ts of using social media responsibly. While we want them to use social media as a tool to open up and see the truth behind those they are interacting with, be mindful not to risk isolating someone in the process.

**State of The Classroom Address:** What is your process of "checking-in" with students? How do you provide students with an update on the direction of the class? I have found it useful to set aside instructional time (does not have to be much) to provide students with a State of the Class address every grading period. In this address, we review goals established at the beginning of the grading period and the steps we took--as a class--to meet those goals. We celebrate all the successes that we had (individually and collectively) and discuss any missed marks we had in class. We also use this time to talk about the direction we are headed as a class and review our long-term goal for the school year. Closing out, we establish new goals for the marking period and discuss the steps and strategies that we will implement to accomplish our marking period goals. If you notice, when talking about the State of the Class, it is a WE thing, not an I thing. It is a conversation of reflection that I facilitate while encouraging students to participate actively. My role is to pose thought-provoking questions and then allow my students to lead the way in the conversation through best practices of discussion, such as think-pair-share, graffiti walls, and post-discussion written reflections. What I enjoy most about our State of the Classroom addresses is that they get real, and I encourage my students to be authentic. I am there for them and help them accomplish their personal and academic goals. These addresses are a real-time of self/class reflections, but most importantly, it is a time to show students that we are on this journey together.

# FOUR

# A LEARNING ENVIRONMENT THAT MEETS THE NEEDS OF ALL OF MY STUDENTS

---

*"When I walk into a room, I do not want to feel ashamed for what I am not but be inspired to become who I am."*

ME

---

I was not attracted to any school because my schools were not attracted to me. I entered spaces that expected me to give them my all but showed no concern about what I needed them to provide to me. My teachers spoke at me and about me but never really talked to me. They encouraged me to attend school, but I was missing from the classroom even when I was present. I had thoughts I wanted to share with the world, but my voice was silenced even when I was not told to be quiet. I acted out because there was so much that I could no longer hold inside. I loved reading, writing, and problem-solving. However, I could not connect to what I was being told to read and could not write in a way that set me free. All the problems that I had to solve involved numbers. I pride myself on being a visual person. When I think back to the places I spent the most time in, I recall broken desks, straight rows, and white walls. A place that should have represented freedom resembled a prison.

The bright California sun shined in my classrooms. Most days, that was the only thing that kept me awake. I struggled with trying to self-manage my ADHD and was too afraid to tell anyone that I could not concentrate on one thing at one time. I needed to be up, out, and putting my hands on things, but that was not an option. My brain would jump from one thought to another. When I could not doodle or talk, I would go to sleep...right there on the front row. Getting kicked out of class was a blessing to me because, finally, I was free! If I did not leave campus, I would roam the school looking for someone to talk or something that would entertain me. When I returned to the classroom, it felt like going back into a jail cell in a foreign country. I felt like a stranger in my own home.

The thoughts, they just kept coming and coming and coming. But I had to deal with them because no one cared to know them. My ADHD turned into anxiety, which would then turn into depression. What triggered these emotions when it came to school? I was forced to be in an environment that did not teach, recognize, or promote anything that spoke to my social, emotional, or cultural needs. This environment made me feel ashamed to be me and forced me to stuff everything that made me who I was on the inside of me just so that I could "fit in." I got tired of being what others wanted me to be. I was still trying to figure out the real me. It was a struggle trying to process the new emotions that I was experiencing. So, in the broad California daylight, I walked right out of the front gates of the school and never looked back.

I see many students today who suffer from severe cases of ADHD, anxiety, depression, and overall trauma as a result of their upbringing and home environment. They enter into our learning spaces and become consumed with trying to control their thoughts and emotions to stay focused. I see students who enter classrooms and feel unwelcomed and unsafe because of the unknown. I see students entering classes where the environment of the room makes them feel isolated from everything and everyone around them. They feel invisible and forced to suppress anything that may make them feel different. I see students who walk the halls of the schools feeling that they do not fit in the campus or the culture of the school. They see their teachers, administrators, and peers, but they wonder, do others see them? When they are tired of feeling invisible and can no longer tolerate or cope with the environment, they begin to explore their options elsewhere.

## What We Do Not Say Speaks Louder Than What We Do Say

Creating a learning environment that speaks to the needs of all of our students means we must first recognize all of our students. Not only do we acknowledge them by name, but we must accept them by culture, community, and anything else that might be important to them. During my time in the classroom, students expressed feelings of being unrecognized or excluded from the curriculum and learning environments that are supposed to help them grow. If we take an in-depth look at the lessons we design and learning spaces we create, they are reflective of who we are. They reinforce our cultural beliefs, values, and hegemonic traditions. In most cases, they lack diversity and authenticity and are not reflective of the students we have or what we want them to become. Many students enter our classroom and schools and see what is important to us, but what is not essential to them. They hear what we want them to know and learn the skills that we think they are capable of learning. The appearance of our classrooms is vital because entry into this space triggers warning signals in our students' brains. These signals will tell them if our classes are safe spaces to enter or not. Our classrooms and the vibe established when we meet students at the door lets them know if they can trust us or not. When our classroom doors are open, our students should be eager to enter and build meaningful connections with the people inside of these rooms. However, some of our learning environments do not say, "enter, I am a haven where you will be allowed to grow into who you are meant to be." Our classrooms do not say, "I respect you, I respect your culture, or I respect the community that you represent."

Multicultural decor, the celebration of multicultural holidays, and using stories and role-playing are great for creating a welcoming space for students from urban communities. Song, dance, and games are wonderful additions to the classroom, as well. However, when creating an environment to meet the needs of all students, the aforementioned is not enough. They only meet the surface and shallow cultural needs of our students. To get what we are teaching to stick, we must get down to the deeply-rooted cultural needs of our students. Here is where we develop trust in our students, and our students grab onto everything we are trying to extend to them. Do not get me wrong; meeting the surface and shallow needs of our students are essential. But we cannot stop there as we seek to grow what Zaretta Hammond (2015) calls, in *Culturally Responsive Teaching and the Brain*, a Culture Tree in our classrooms. Nurturing the inward parts of students' culture, such as their decision-making, concept of self, world view, definitions of kinship, and notions of fairness will make our focus on everything else be more meaningful. It will allow us to connect with our students truly. So, how do you get to the deep level of your students? One word: RESEARCH.

Now, that does not mean that you run down to the local Barnes and Noble or Half-Priced Books and purchase all the academic literature on culture in the classroom or teaching in urban spaces (but there is great scholarship on Culturally Responsive Pedagogy and Reality Pedagogy that is a must for all educators). The academic scholarship is essential. Understanding the positionality of your students, self-reflection, and engaging in what Christopher Emdin (2011) refers to as "cogenerative dialogues"--teachers and students engaging in a "critical deconstruction" of what happens in the classroom in an egalitarian manner--, will help you learn more about their needs than an academic text will provide. Learning the needs of your students will not happen overnight. As well, trying to figure out their individual needs might cause you to wrestle with emotions that you feel inept to handle. But keep hope, because patience, consistency, and reflection will take you in a positive direction.

When envisioning spaces that meet students' needs, be careful not to send a message that we care only about meeting part of that need. We must be mindful not to focus on their social, emotional, or learning needs without addressing their cultural needs. Our classrooms should say to students, loud and clear that we care about them as individuals, and we care about them as members of larger communities. They should also know that in our classrooms, every part of them will be carefully cared for and nurtured to grow, survive, and thrive. For this to happen, we must re-examine our learning spaces, lesson plans, seating arrangements, and the conversations that occur and do not occur in our classrooms. Whatever is present in our learning spaces, we must question its purpose and what we are seeking to accomplish from its presence. Whatever is missing, let's ask ourselves why and aim to make relevant changes immediately.

When reflecting on your learning environment, think about your favorite eating establishment and what initially attracted you to it. If you are anything like me, you first check out its reviews on Google or Yelp. After checking out the reviews, you then check out the distance of the restaurant from your home or current location. After loading up a family of six (wait, that's just me), you then travel to your destination, anticipating if it is going to be crowded or not. When you first enter, you scan the room and the decor to get a sense of the vibe. Although your focus might be on the restaurant's appearance, you are most concerned about how you were greeted and made to feel when you entered. Were you made to feel welcomed, and were the staff excited to have you there? Or, did you feel like a burden on the staff and just another customer they had to serve?

Another thing most of us tune into is our inner security system and the signals it set off inside of us. If we are alerted to enter, that is because the initial environment and greeting said: "go for it, give it a shot!" But, most of us have been to places where our eternal warning systems screamed at us to run fast because something about the restaurant was sketchy. Me, I look at the seating arrangements and its relationship to the restaurant and other patrons. While I like for my family to have space to enjoy our time and meal, I also want to be close enough to others to feel a sense of community. I am a conversationalist, so I also like to be close enough to another table to spark up a conversation. I do not want to be told where to sit because while the restaurant may have drawn me in, that's not the case for some of the patrons. However, if I am directed to sit next to unfamiliar faces, I tread lightly but with an open mind. While dining, I am actively doing two things (well, actually more than that because I'm the mom of four): listening and observing. I'm paying attention to the music played and the conversations taking place. As well, I'm checking out the decor, connections being made, and the body language of the staff when not in the direct view of customers. At this moment, I am considering if this place is for me or not. Does it represent values I hold personally, and does it attempt to include my culture into its decor theme? Some would say that this does not matter because the restaurant is about the food. If the establishment wants to gain a loyal customer, it will take more than food to communicate that they welcome, value, and look forward to my return. When the food arrives, I should be just as excited about the food as I am about the establishment. When I receive my dish, I first look at its presentation. Yes, presentation matters! When I take my first bite, I am tasting it for seasoning, authenticity.

I am also testing to see if I am receiving their best made just to my liking and hunger needs. While I am eating, I am still observing the vibe in the room. The food is what brought our family out, but it is not what will keep us in. While we are eating, I like for the managers or servers to come and check on us. Without prompting, they should see if we have any needs. As we prepare to leave, I enjoy being asked about my meal and inspired to "come again." When I get into the car, I want to have great conversations with my family about the food and begin planning our next trip. When I get home, I want to go back to Google or Yelp and give the establishment an overall five-star raving review about the experience that I just had.

Just like we expect restaurants to provide us with five-star service and breathtaking dishes, we should give the students five-star service and meals tailored to their needs. Like we would desire, when they enter our learning spaces, they should feel welcomed, valued, and encouraged to return. The service they receive should be individualized and tailored to their needs. Their meal, which is the reason why they decided to visit your restaurant, should be cooked to perfection. This standard of perfection is not what you deem acceptable but a heaping that will satisfy them for the moment and long after. Be mindful, however, that while the food could be the best in the world, it will not keep a customer coming back to more. If the service, environment, and overall vibe of the restaurant do not communicate to a customer that they belong or speak to their deeper needs as an individual, they will not return. The content that we teach is the food that will satisfy their immediate hunger needs. The teacher presents the material tailored in a way that meets the individual learner. BUT THE FOOD WILL NOT GUARANTEE THEY RETURN. For a student to return, the teacher's five-star service must happen at the door. The vibe of our classroom must say that ALL students are welcomed to come as they are. In our rooms, we speak to their deep inner needs, and we structure our classroom to do so as well. When students are in a space designed to provide them with the best experience ever, every part of them should feel as if they matter. They know they matter because we have communicated that to them both verbally and non-verbally. When they leave the classroom, we want them anticipating the next time they will return, and we want them to share the amazing experience with those that matter the most to them. If your classroom was into the service industry, what would your Google or Yelp review say about the way your establishment does business?

## If the Walls Could Talk

One of my favorite things to do is to sit in coffee shops. I love to listen to all of the stories that are being told by the people sitting around. I hear stories of success, stories of failure, and stories that include all the ups and downs of life. These stories include laughs, smiles, tears, and hugs. They connect people and allow individuals to let go and let it all out. Stories are compelling because we all have a story to tell. In many cultures, stories are what connect one generation to the next. They often shape how we view, understand, and operate in society. Our stories have power, meaning, and so much depth. Hearing or telling a great story among others can be thus freeing to one's soul.

I love hearing and telling stories in my classroom because they are an effective way to connect with students and transmit information in a form that will have a lasting impact. However, the most important stories told in our classrooms are not the ones that we hold, but the ones that our students are longing to tell. The stories that our students possess can tell us a lot about them and how we can tailor our instruction and classrooms to meet their individual needs. Their stories can be empowering to them, us, and, most importantly, their peers. How are you allowing your students to find freedom through their stories and giving them a voice through the conversations had and the tales shared? Our classrooms should be a space where intentional discussions take place daily. What I mean by intentional is that every conversation takes us on a journey of discovery where we learn about ourselves, and we learn about others. Every student should be encouraged and supported during the mental trip in hopes that they leave enlightened by what they learned and heard.

Like great folklores, every story shared in a classroom teaches us about culture, customs, and generations before us. They are our eyes to the world and the souls of others. These stories contain powerful and meaningful lessons, but not sharing these lessons will not impart wisdom to others. Teachers should not be the only ones giving understanding and teaching students lessons because we are not the holders of all knowledge. In a previous chapter, I spoke earlier about the importance of conversations in the classroom when it came to building lessons with students. I am talking about it again because the conversations that happen in our classes are what make our classrooms. How can we educate students according to their needs if we do not hear their voices? How can we inspire them if we do not know their source of inspiration? How can we speak life into them without giving them a platform to speak?

Finding out what a person needs to survive, thrive, and be successful in life starts with a conversation. If we are not having conversations in our classrooms (I mean REAL discussions), we can never honestly know what our students need. How can you help a flower grow, if you never take a trip into the garden to see if it is still alive and what you can do to further its growth? We are gardeners, and our classroom is a flower bed with a variety of beautiful flowers blooming. While mixed, all of these flowers have different needs to survive. You cannot treat them all the same. Yet, how will you know how to handle the bud if you have not intentionally studied the flower? Studies have shown that talking to plants can help them grow faster, so why think differently when it comes to the spaces of our classrooms?

I was a rose fighting to grow from underneath the pavement, but I found a crack that gave me sunlight--a little glimpse of hope. Someone witnessed my fight and stopped. The words we exchanged became the water that I needed to nourish my roots that settled beneath the concrete. Conversations we shared spoke life into both of us, and from them, I continued to grow taller and taller. My petals began to bloom when I noticed the power that was in me. The words gave me life, a voice, and told me to grow. And grow, I did. My water was a teacher, my peers, and the conversations we were allowed to have in a safe space, and, from there, I learned to breathe fresh air in the four walls of that room.

If we sit and look around our classrooms, the best storyteller in the room would not be our students or us, but the walls. The walls cannot tell their story, but can only sit and listen to all the stories told and created. When I sit and look at the walls in my classroom, I often think to myself, if these walls could talk, what would they say? What would they say about me as the teacher, mentor, and friend? What would they say about my students? What would they say about the relationships developed in that classroom and the missed opportunities? What would they say about the space they enclosed and what they have witnessed throughout the school year? Would they say they saw an environment where real learning was happening, love given, and life lessons learned? Did they observe, in action, a learning environment that welcomed and educated all the students that entered? Or, did they witness faces that soon became long-lost memories that they wished would return?

Most importantly, what would they say about what they heard, and the lives transformed from the stories that were told? Would they have much to share or shake their heads in despair? What would they say? Let's give our wall words to share by providing all students a voice to speak.

## The Skin They Are in Is Not Who They Are

Arian came to me frustrated with school because she was "tired of being treated black." She explained that in her classes, which were all advanced placement or dual enrollment, her teachers overlooked her. They undermined her words, and she was confident that it was because all her teachers saw was her brown skin. She was tired of her teachers' shocked responses when she gave the right answer to a question. Or, them treating her as if she was the spokesperson for all things diversity. Arian was gifted and talented in math, science, English, and social studies. This information was in her academic file. However, she felt her teachers could not see past her skin to know that she was capable of accomplishing "rigorous" tasks thrown at her condescendingly. Despite her academic potential, Arian lost her drive and admitted to "becoming what they wanted her to be." They viewed her as unmotivated, so why show up to class on time or at all? She was considered loud, so loud is what she became. Her instructors and peers addressed issues involving minorities with a condescending caution. When those "sensitive" topics arose, Arian gave them the anger and raw emotions expected from a student of color. She became everything she felt her white teachers and peers assumed she was.

Chuck grew up in a trailer park on the south side of his city. From elementary school to high school, he was a minority in school. His white face and blue eyes stood out in a sea of black and brown skin, but to "Chucky," this was normal. Amongst his friends, he felt like himself, but in the classroom, he was placed on a pedestal, and he knew it was because of his whiteness. He loved listening to hip-hop, R&B, and gangsta-rap like NWA, which spoke to his identity and shaped his worldview. He viewed his black and brown peers as his brothers, sisters, and cousins and empathized with them because he had seen the realities of racism in his community. His friends knew of his struggles, and he witnessed theirs. From their shared hardships, they grew a solid bond rooted in the way they saw the world. Teachers spoke to and treated Chuck differently, and he hated it because he knew his whiteness is what made him "better." While he had the potential to excel, he knew his friends did too, but teachers did not push and challenged them the way they challenged Chuck. Chuck thought and knew that some of his friends were more capable than him and grew to despise those who chose not to see it. Chuck was raised not to see color, but as he became older, he had no choice but to take off the glasses that blinded him. Chuck had academic, emotional, and social needs that caused him to struggle in school. He had a home life that no one understood, but maybe his friends. In school, his needs went overlooked because of the assumption that Chuck had support and resources at home and did not need any assistance from the school. Chuck was placed at the top of a social hierarchy when he did not want to be, so he jumped down and began to cry out for help in all of the wrong ways.

Our goal is to create a learning environment that speaks to the needs of all students. To accomplish this goal, we must get to know and begin to see our students for who they are and not the skin that they are wearing. Does this mean to stick to the notion of being "colorblind?" No, because seeing the color of our students helps us to see our own biases, stereotypes, and assumptions that limit our students in our classrooms and expands what Gloria Ladson-Billings (2006) refers to as the "education debt" that many students of color, in inner-city schools, are paying for as a result of historical, economic, socio-political, and moral components that have denied people of color full equality in America. Seeing our students for who they are means focusing on creating an environment where biases, assumptions, and stereotypes do not exist. In this environment, equitable opportunities for learning are the only things actively present. In this space, we allow our students to have a voice in what they learn, how they learn, and how they can demonstrate mastery. Our classrooms should speak to and educate according to the surface, shallow, and deep cultural needs of students and not the ones we force on them. What we teach is rigorous and standard-based but differentiated and applicable to all students. Our instruction should not make assumptions on a student's ability to demonstrate mastery or not because of the color of their skin or assumed cultural characteristic. However, our instruction is liberating when our students can learn more about themselves from what and how we teach.

Students should have agency in our classrooms, and we should allow them to be hands-on in the curriculum designing processes to ensure that curriculums are culturally responsive, realistic, anti-racist, enriching, diversified, and differentiated. In our classes, students like Aarian are supported, encouraged, and challenged. Not because of her "gifted and talented" label but because we have studied her. We know that she thrives off of being tested and is empowered by conversations that make her feel valued and welcomed as a young black woman. In our classes, Chuck's needs are not assumed and overlooked. But, like Aarian, we have examined all students to the point where we know that hip-hop and great stories will make Chuck's eyes light up because that is what surrounds him daily. He loves interacting with his friends and is disgusted by any privilege he receives because of this whiteness. We have studied Chuck well enough to know that for him to thrive in our learning space, he needs a great deal of freedom with a little hint of support. However, as he succeeds, he will fight for those around him to thrive, as well.

So, how do we create a learning environment that meets the needs of ALL students? It's simple, study every student that enters your room. Like you would prepare for a test, listen to their lectures, watch their interactions, interact with them, and take copious notes. This preparation cannot happen while sitting at your desk, standing behind a podium, or performing in a one-person show. It can only occur when there is freedom and flexibility in the classroom, and the teacher is willing to step off the stage and step into the role of the practitioner. They are carefully studying their students and reflectively thinking at the same time. From their thoughts, reflective judgments are made based on what they have observed. Educators are taking risks, and their boldness takes the place of their fear. They relinquish the control of the classroom to the students and use the feedback of the students to plan their next steps. ALL students create a learning environment that speaks to the needs of ALL students. It welcomes them, educates them, influences them, and then it INSPIRES them. Just sit back and relax; they have it all under control.

## Classroom Strategies to Create A Learning Environment That Meets the Needs of All Students

**DIY Classroom**: When you look around at your classroom, is it a reflection of you, or is it a reflection of your students? Do you see what is important to them, and what is important to you? A DIY Classroom is a great way to get to know what is essential to your students and decorate your classroom at the same time. However, this will not happen overnight. Yet, if you look on the bright side, you do not have to stress about having your class decorated by the first day of school. Begin by having students bring or design their favorite poster to hang on the wall. You can also start by having each student write one quote or word that describes them. Or, have them capture a photo of something they admire about their community and the people in it. When they bring their products to class, have them present them to the class. Follow up presentations with a facilitated discussion about the inspiration behind students' work. Then, hang their pieces of art on the walls and allow the walls to grow from there (in an orderly fashion). Each week or grading cycle, have students bring something to present to the class, and after presentations, you have a wall decorating ceremony. Allowing your students to design their own learning space will give students a greater connection and responsibility to the classroom. It is also a great way to meet the surface, shallow, and deep needs of students without you making any assumptions. As you transition into covering content, leave a space for students' artwork and need-to-knows. However, in the same manner, allow students to create, present, and decide what is important to them and necessary to be presented in the classroom. Great conversations and life lessons will come out of working together to design your classroom.

The role of the teacher is to facilitate what goes up and comes down. At this point, use your professional judgment. We want our classes to be a space that is welcoming to all students. If a student attempts to include something hurtful or inappropriate, you must use this as a teachable moment to educate the class on creating inclusive spaces rooted in equity. You will not regret allowing your students to design your classroom each year. During this process, they will evolve into active participants whose voices have shaped their learning environment. Wait, did I already mention that you do not have to decorate!

**Flexible Seating**: My favorite restaurants are the ones when I am allowed to sit where I choose. When I enter a restaurant, I have the opportunity to feel for the vibe and decide my seat from there. Some days I am feeling super social, and other days, I want to enjoy a nice quiet meal with my family. Students explore the same way. Some days are good, and some days they might want to kick back and be in the environment. Does your learning space provide them with options of where and when they can sit? I know there is tons of buzz about flexible seating arrangements. When you see all the awesomely designed classrooms, you're thinking, "that's great, but who is going to pay for it? I can't even get my school to buy pencils."

Contrary to popular belief, flexible seating arrangements do not have to involve fancy chairs on bean bags. Your classroom should be flexible and free. Now, what it will require is for you to ditch the rows and predetermined small groups. All you need to do is create safe spaces for students to collaborate, if in the mood, or problem-solve on the solo if that is what they desire to do for the day. Your standard desks, a few chairs, and a couple of rugs can turn into the perfect flexible seating arrangement. Your classroom may even work outside on some days. You have to be flexible in how you view the structure of your class. If you cannot decide how to arrange your classroom, include it in your DIY days. Then, allow your students to switch it up for you now and then.

**Weekly Self-Assessments**: I learned about Weekly Self-Assessments in one of my graduate classes after reading Alfie Kohn's *The Case Against*

*Grades*. The professor who was instructing the course did not agree in assigning us grades. Instead, she guided us in reflecting over our week in the class and allowed us to decide our points earned based on our demonstration of learning. What I enjoyed about weekly self-assessment is the weight lifted from worrying about the grade I was going to make on assignments. From this strategy, I had the opportunity to reflect on my work, and then I made the final decision on how many points I received for an assignment. If the instructor agreed with the points I believed I earned, she would award me those points. If her evaluation of my performance did not match my points, or she felt I deserved something different, she would engage me in a conversation about my grades until we came to a consensus. Weekly Self-Assessments empowered me and also allowed me the freedom to learn and suck-up all the good from the course. The weekly self-assessments stuck with me to the point that I incorporated them into my classroom. However, it did not happen without trial and error. It was a struggle for students at first, but with guidance and patience, they came to appreciate them. I saw learning happen differently. Like me, students were free and got to tailor learning to their liking. I also noticed that my students felt empowered and more accountable for their learning. Students enjoyed not worrying about the grades they received. They also enjoyed the encouragement of developing a growth mindset when reflecting on their submitted work and conferencing with me about how they could grow as learners.

**Community Stations**: Dr. Christopher Emdin presented this strategy in a TED Talk on Reality pedagogy. When I heard of it, I thought to myself, "WOW...why haven't I thought of using this before." Learning stations are becoming a popular trend in education. While the content might connect with students while at the station, is the station itself representative or connecting with students? When creating a learning environment, are we placing our classrooms in the context of students' communities? Are we showing appreciation for what makes their communities so unique and beautiful to our students? To create a class that celebrates and shows understanding and appreciation of students' communities, try naming areas or stations in your classrooms after streets of students' neighborhoods or the roads that surround the school. Instead of instructing a student to go to "Station 1," try telling them to go to the "Bishop Arts District" or "Fair Park," which are both major cultural centers in the Dallas-Ft. Worth area. For students, it brings their communities into the classroom and shows your acknowledgment of the spaces they frequent. It further transforms the class from your space to a more student-friendly environment that is reflective of students' reality outside of the school. It's something so simple yet something that can be so powerful.

**This is What We Do**: How do you and your students celebrate successes or communicate with each other in the classroom? When they show mastery of a concept or complete a difficult task, what do you all do? When it calls for it, how do you get your students to get HYPE? For my students and me, we hit the Whoa, or whatever else they are doing in the streets or at the pep rallies. It might be a complicated dance move, an individualized handshake, or a common saying of "that's what's up." But it is what we do in 2122. What we do is not something decided by me and something that I do not initiate. However, after building relationships with students and bonds of trust, it is something that I allow to happen and grow on its own. Finding something that bonds you with your students is an earned privilege that cannot be demanded or required. As well, be mindful not to enter your students' space uninvited. What I mean by this is that we must be careful to assume that our students want us in their worlds without their permission. It's like being on a first-name basis with them in a sense. It comes as a result of relationship and trust-building. When your students are ready, they will let you know. Start by greeting them at the door and welcoming them with a smile. When the walls come down, and the relationships are solid, soon you'll be giving slap, slap, daps, with a fist pump and a YAH!

# FIVE

# LOYALTY TO MY STUDENTS AND THEIR OVERALL SUCCESS

*"If you will not die for us, you cannot ask us to die for you."*

JACQUELINE CAREY

I t was hard for me to find people that I could trust and develop solid relationships with them, especially adults. I was very cautious about who I opened up to in fear of being judged or rejected. I held a lot of stuff inside that enhanced the eternal trauma I was already experiencing because I was scared the truth would turn people away. Building relationships was hard for me, growing up, because I could not risk opening up, giving my all, and someone running away with it. However, when I did find those who "held me down," the loyalty was reciprocated. "Trust no one but ride for those who ride for you," became my motto. Growing up in the streets, I saw too many people get played, and if my momma and daddy played me, what exempted me from the hurt and disappointment of others? Loyalty was hard to come by, but when you found a circle of friends that was solid, you stuck with them and proved your dedication to them no matter what. Showing your commitment often had risks, but people who had your back surrounded you.

Growing up in South Central gave you no option but to have a reliable and loyal team. However, you had to learn that everyone on your team was not always trustworthy and faithful as you were. Many of the friends I surrounded myself with were people I grew up with, but that did not stay the same as we got older. Your friends today could become your enemies tomorrow, especially when they began riding with people who were the "other" in your eyes. Finding someone who would not turn on you, especially when you needed them the most, redefined what it meant to be loyal.

When I think of a loyal person, I think of someone who will go above and beyond for me with nothing to gain. They desire to see me accomplish my dreams. When I felt I had nothing to offer and was unworthy of their friendship, they still stuck by my side. They cheered me on even in my misery. A loyal person is one who, despite the direction and journey you decide to travel, they are present and consistent. They may not agree with every decision that you make. However, through the good and bad, you could count on them to hold you accountable. They will have your back, pick you up, dust you off, and encourage you to try again.

For me, loyalty was hard to come by in the classroom, especially when the going got tough. When it comes to teaching students in urban communities, loyalty, trust, and respect go hand and hand. I had many teachers who talked a good game about being there when I needed them but turned their back when I became "too much." They would start a process with me, but when I gave up in the middle of the process, they gave up too. If they did not give up on me early on, what they were doing for "poor little old me" became the topic of every conversation in the breakroom. I became the poster child of pity amongst other teachers when I was not looking for a superhero. I went to school looking for guidance from those knowledgeable about questions my family members could not answer. But, when I sensed a teacher becoming frustrated or disingenuous, I gave up on myself. I did not want to be someone's experiment; I just wanted to be pushed beyond the limits I placed on myself. I also did not want someone's pity. I just needed a sense of direction and for someone to have my back apart from the support I found in the streets. I needed an advocate when I could not advocate for myself. And, most importantly, I needed someone brave enough to be my voice. When I could not speak for myself, they would speak up and say what needed to be said, not what everyone else wanted to hear.

Recently, I have witnessed too many teachers who are obsessed with being Twitter-worthy to the point where it is self-serving and no longer about expanding their learning network for their students. As a result, they are no longer acting in the best interest of their students. Their loyalty is not to their students, but the school, to themselves, and their professional careers. They are loyal to their content, lesson plans, and scope and sequence and would instead drop the ball on their students rather than miss a beat. Their students know and see that they are just pawns in a chess game and question giving their all in the classroom. Loyalty to our students is vital in our classes and should guide every-thing that we do. If we claim that we are there for students, then we need to be there for the students. Our loyalty cannot just be with the well-behaved students who are making good grades, but all students.

Every student that enters our room should know, automatically, that we--their teachers--will have their backs to the end of time. They should know that when the going gets tough, we will get tougher and continue to fight with them and for them. From every meeting we have regarding their success, we genuinely speak on their behalf and become their voice. We speak up for them when they cannot or will not speak up for them-selves. Loyalty means that we ensure that they are provided with equi-table curriculum, resources, situations, and materials to ensure their success, even if we have to go get, or create, them ourselves. Loyalty is us giving them our all and expecting nothing in return, and when we see them derailing, we leave the track to go after them. Loyal teachers take risks for students and exemplify what it means to have their backs even during uncomfortable times.

## Loyalty Might Cause You to Deviate from The Plan, and It's Okay

I still remember the first day I sat in a staffing meeting, as a new teacher, to prepare for an Admission, Review, and Dismall (ARD) meeting for one of my students. In this meeting, the campus principal briefed teachers, counselors, and representatives on the parent, student, and how we should handle ourselves in this meeting. Since this was my very first ARD meeting, I was more observational in the staff meeting to gain a feel for how ARDs and 504-meetings worked. Coming out of an alternative certification program, I did not have any background knowledge of my role in an ARD or 504-meeting. I was learning as we went along. In the staffing meeting for the ARD, we discussed the student and their specific behaviors and learning needs in our classes. In my opinion, this student was not a poor performing student. From my observations of him and his work, and interactions with him, it was evident that this student required some academic support. He needed someone to push him in reaching his full potential. When asked to share our observations on the student, all of his classroom teachers agreed that he needed specific accommodations and modifications. However, we were cautioned to be careful of agreeing to these accommodations and placing them on paper. The principal believed these accommodations would give the parent--who was already problematic--more leverage to be in constant contact with teachers and the school. To be clear, we were encouraged to make the accommodations we saw necessary in our classrooms. However, by putting them on paper, we were opening Pandora's box.

Still taking things in, I nodded in agreement to be mindful of what accommodations and modifications were agreed upon and returned to my classroom. Several days before our official ARD meeting, I had the chance to continue to observe and interact with the student of focus. As I witnessed him shine in some areas and struggle in others, I began to question whose needs we were seeking to serve. Were we trying to help the student, his parents, or the school? As a new teacher, I began to see educators in a different light. This student, in particular, was a student of color who had, in his lifetime, experienced a severe amount of trauma that was well known by all of his teachers and school officials. We sat in meetings and talked about equality and equity in education, but behind closed doors, we debated if we should provide this particular student with equitable opportunities because of a difficult parent.

Entering the ARD meeting, I was very nervous and uncomfortable. This anxiety came from the relationship I had with the student and seeing him during his struggle. While I was already attempting to accommodate him in my classroom, I started to see the necessity of having something in writing. Official accommodations will hold others accountable for providing equitable experiences in their classrooms. It was heartbreaking to realize that educators would turn their backs to a student to avoid dealing with a difficult parent. I could not stand it. Whatever the parent's motivations were, we could not be sure. However, they had every right to request that their child had support systems in place to ensure they had a fair shot at being successful.

Before the meeting, I felt the need to conference with the students about the needs they thought they had. In this meeting, I encouraged them to voice their needs because the meeting was about them, not about ego-tripping adults. However, when we all sat around the conference room table, I noticed that the student became intimidated. He was intimidated by adult faces in the room and was a child who did not know how to advocate for himself. It was at that moment that I questioned who my loyalty was with--with my student or with my school?

I could not sit back and continue to nod in agreement as adults sat around a table and talked about the student without the student. Yes, he was physically there, but it became evident that he had mentally checked out and had had enough of these meetings. Because I knew what it felt like to yearn for someone to step up and be my voice when I could not speak up for myself, I had to speak up for the student. As uncomfortable as it was, I had to be the voice of opposition, yet the voice of reason. In a room full of adults, the student needed to see that someone would put their ego aside and bring the meeting back to the focus of what we were there for, the student. Somebody had to have his back, especially when it was up against a wall.

When it comes to the needs of our students, loyalty will cause you to deviate from the plan, and it is okay. Just remember that when it is in the best interest of the student, it will always sort itself out when done genuinely. It may not always be popular, but we must act on their behalf in the manner that we would want someone to do for our children or us. I have observed that many educators struggle with being loyal to their students because it's somebody else's child. In their eyes, the decision they make regarding that student has no direct effect on their lives, so why should it matter? It matters because the values that we instill into our students now are the values that they will stick to in the future. Loyalty is merely doing right by a person with nothing to gain from it. Loyalty is rooted in integrity and your ability to be honest and live honest in front of others. I have heard many educators say, "well, they should have learned that at home." Yet, sadly, that is not always the case. We have many students who enter our classrooms with no sense of loyalty at all because they have never experienced someone being loyal to them. When they leave our schools, they take this with them into the world and build a mistrust of everyone, especially those in a position of power and influence. Supposed allies did not act on their behalf when needed, so they do not know how to act on behalf of others with integrity when called.

Showing students that we will stand up for them even when it means going against the grain means more to them than we know. From experience, stepping up in defense of a student when they were in the middle of a tug of war transformed the relationship I had with that student and even yielded great academic results. When this student was shy and reserved around others, he was lively and engaging in my presence. He witnessed my loyalty in action and grew confidence in knowing that I would protect him from adults and his peers. Loyalty to our students is a MUST. It is from our commitment that they slowly remove any internal barriers that might hinder them. It is from our dedication that they receive the inspiration needed to step out. They will test the world because they know that someone will be there to catch them when they fall.

## Meet Our Students Where They Are and Enjoy Them in That Moment

When I entered any classroom, I had tons to offer and contribute to any learning environment, but I presented it differently. I prided myself on being "street" because of the many life lessons and experiences I had gained from running the "streets." As mentioned throughout the book, I was outspoken, creative, and possessed a tremendous amount of leadership skills. I did not mind taking the initiative and was a real risk-taker. In the early 2000s, I was the epitome of a 21st-century student; I just looked a little different. However, when I entered many learning spaces, there was more focus placed on what I was not than what I was. My rambunctious personality became the focus of, and turn off to, many educators I encountered. They dedicated their time to correcting my improper usage of grammar or policing my "ghettoness." Some teachers did not want much to do with me because I was not "compliant" and refused to conform.

I have encountered many students who have so much to offer but package it differently. Because many of these students exist in a body that is black, brown, or poor, their teachers overlook their qualities. As educators, we have embraced this dangerous narrative--this single-sided story--that you can't be "street" or "hood" and be sophisticated or educated at the same time. Because of this, we devote too much precious energy to dictating the respectability of our students and policing them than we do loving and educating them. Why is this so? Because we do not value or appreciate their cultures or communities. Many educators have demonized their spaces and also demonized the students that come from those spaces. We find it difficult to believe that they would have anything valuable to offer our schools and classrooms if the communities that they come from are detrimental. So, when students from low socioeconomic communities enter our schools, they do so under the scrutiny of educators who have allowed their deficit thinking to blind them. They see their stereotypes, biases, and assumptions of race and poverty but not their students who might be a diamond in the rough.

To meet students where they are, and enjoy them in that moment, we must first know and understand their communities. A good culturally relevant teacher considers themselves members of the community they serve and their teaching as a way to serve their community (Ladson-Billings, 1995). Throughout, this book focuses on the importance of culture and society. A full understanding of the culture of students and their communities is central to understanding the real value that students from urban spaces possess. They are assets to our learning spaces, and we must begin treating them as such. Our knowledge and understanding of their cultures and communities cannot be constructed based on assumptions, stereotypes, or "what we have seen." Our education must come from conversations and interaction with students, families, or community partners and experiences that we have had from situating ourselves in their communities as active participants.

I once worked in a small urban school district in the Dallas Fort Worth (DFW) Metroplex. The population of students was primarily made up of African Americans and Hispanics. When I entered this school, as a new teacher, it had a reputation for being a harsh environment where kids "did not learn," and teachers could not teach. Fresh out of my teacher-certification program, the rumors intimidated me and made me believe that I had to go in--at 23 years old--and rule students with an iron fist. If no one else could get them together, I knew I could, and I would. Getting them into academic shape became my overall mission as I embraced the belief that students of color had to be "fixed" into shape. I entered their space and their community as another person telling them what they needed to do to be taken seriously in the world. Because obviously, their community was not doing what needed to be done to ensure their children were successful in life. Boy, was I wrong? As I grew comfortable with the school, my co-workers, students, and communities, my idea of what the city was changed. I came to realize how blinded to their beauty I had become. Despite how "woke" I thought I was, I used dominant norms to judge their space. This school district was a family and community in every sense of the word. They were a community whose roots ran deep. They had pride in their community and fought to ensure that their children had the best. They were a tight-knit family-oriented community that took care of one another and cheered each other on to greatness. Outsiders saw a troubled school and troubled students, while insiders knew of the future doctors, lawyers, educators, and world-changers that existed in the walls of the schools. In their schools, they saw hope because they once walked the halls and built the walls of the schools. Outsiders saw an athletic powerhouse, but so much more existed. Excellence was in their blood, but the outside world could not see it because of how they packaged their excellence.

I still keep up with many of my former students from my first few years of teaching, and it is their stories that make this section of this chapter so important. Seeing their faces and accomplishments serve as a constant reminder that it is not my place to police the behaviors of my students. Yet, I must embrace them and show them how to use what they possess to capitalize on what the world has to offer. Many of my former students have become great parents, successful lawyers, and doctors. They are great educators, entrepreneurs, mentors, community leaders, and professional athletes who are dominating their industries in their early twenties. Their success is not because of the school "fixing" them, but because of their communities raising them. Yes, they went on to study business, education, or law in college. But their communities instilled in them the drive, persistence, dedication, ingenuity, and leadership skills that they needed to preserve against the odds.

I am hesitant to brag on what my former students have accomplished in life because I only played a small role in it if that. Their accomplishments are a result of what their community valued and instilled in them, which pushed them to blaze trails when others doubted they could. When we look at the faces of the students in our classrooms and attempt to over-analyze and manage their behavior, we must do so with caution. The heart of effective classroom management is not policing the dispositions of our students. Yet, it is engaging them in a way that will allow their hidden potential to shine through. Our expanding cultural competence and understanding of our students' communities can help us build bridges from the community to the classroom. It is not our place to dictate how they navigate or exist in educational spaces, especially when schools are already seen as an "alien and hostile" place for some black and brown students (Ladson-Billings, 1995). We have to allow them to grow freely. My students often told me, "Mrs. Terry, don't worry... I got this!" Now, looking back, they did have it. Many educators refuse to see that their students can handle "this"--making decisions that are best for them-- because of their obsession with how "this" looks and how students' decisions and behaviors align with white mainstream values. Be in the moment with your students and support them as they grow. Don't trust your doings, but trust the values installed in them. When they tell you not to worry about them because "they got this," believe it. A real gardener never focuses on what a rose cannot be but is loyal to watering them with love and compassion because they know what they can grow to become.

## Teachers Can Also Be A "Ride or Die"

A teacher being a "ride or die" is a concept that may take many educators aback because of the everyday usage of the words. "Ride or die" was a phrase that was popular amongst bikers. The expression then became used to describe a female companion, in a relationship, who would do anything for her partner, even if that meant risking her life. For educators, "ride or die" means going above and beyond for students. It is an extension of our loyalty to them.

As a mother, I want the best for my children and my family--mentally, physically, spiritually, and emotionally. I want to ensure that my children have the best. Giving my children the best requires me to make many sacrifices. There are times I have to do things when I do not want to do it or have little strength to do it. For example, because I want my family to have all of me during the day, I wake up extremely early. I rise early, so my children do not have to witness me working on a particular project or grading papers, while they are asking for my attention. When I am with them, I am all in, and when I am not with them, I am seeking ways that I can grow as a mother for them. In my home, I am my family's "ride or die" as they know I will continuously have their backs when no one else does.

I often hear educators brag about how their students are their "children." While this statement flies loosely off their lips and floods my social media streams, I often question to what extent are these statements said in truth? An educator treating a child as their own is going above and beyond to give students their best. Just as they would want for their children. They give them the best classroom, the best instruction, and the best lessons. THEIR BEST. Unfortunately, while hearing educators refer to students as "their children" or "their babies," it often sounds good, but the proof is not in the pudding. Being honest with ourselves, some of us are guilty of providing an education to other people's kids that would be unacceptable for our kids. Some of us work in schools that we would not even want our children to attend. So, are they like our children or babies? Or does it make us feel good and look good when those words roll off our lips?

As my children got older and began attending the local public schools, it was time for me to have an honest conversation with myself--as a parent and as an educator. I toiled day and night to ensure that my children were well taken care of and had the best opportunities when outside of my home. When they entered any place of learning, I was extremely involved in the school, sometimes overly hands-on with their teachers. I was not hesitant to demand the best for my children when it came to the quality of their teachers and the learning that was taking place in their classrooms. However, I was hypocritical when it came to my classes. I shunned the "helicopter" parent and frowned upon PDs that could help me grow professionally. I am also guilty of popping in a movie or showing a documentary when I convinced myself that I did not have the energy to teach that day. Yeah! These actions are coming from the parent who questioned the learning objectives that caused my son to struggle. If I felt necessary, I would challenge the teacher's role in the classroom when it did not meet my standards of being orderly and engaging. I have even made suggestions to my son's teachers on improving instruction in their classroom but was not willing to take my advice. But I prided myself on my students calling me "Momma Terry" and me "loving them like they were my own," But, did I?

Being a ride or die teacher means that our classrooms and schools are worthy enough for our children. We are playing an active role in ensuring that teaching and learning that takes place in our building is supreme for everyone's children. We hold ourselves accountable for providing our students with the quality of education we demand our own children receive. We treat other people's children--the ones we call our babies--the way we would want our children treated. Reforming our practices can only come by having a growth mindset, continuous self-reflection, and constant reflective thinking and judgments taking place.

Having a growth mindset means that we are continuously seeking out ways to grow personally and professionally for our students and schools, putting our self-interest aside. We are attending PDs, participating in PLNs, and making every effort to study and get to know our students. We know their learning and love language just like we know that of our children. We are in constant pursuit of opportunities to grow. And, no matter how long we have been in the profession, we are not afraid or too prideful to step outside our comfort zones to grow professionally. When the opportunities present themselves to bring new experiences and resources to our students--especially those that will prepare them for the future--we are quick to seize those opportunities. We do all of this because we want our students to have the best.

Reviewing lessons for improvement is a must, and if the lesson needs to be dumped and re-designed, we do not mind doing so. Every learning experience is relevant to the times and the needs of our students. You craft every learning opportunity with love like that favorite recipe our children enjoy. When our students leave our classrooms, they feel confi-dent in their ability to take on the world because we have prepared them for that very moment. We grow tired from studying up and researching the latest trends in education because our students too deserve us during the midnight oil or rising with the chickens. And, the same way we demand our precious babies to be treated--with love, respect, compassion, equity, and equality --we uphold these values with children entrusted to us. Reflection is a must because we want to be the best for our students. However, we do not just stop at the thought of our strengths or areas of weakness. However, we are intentional about improving and growing in those areas. We maximize our strengths by doing everything we can to ensure that we stay fresh and surround ourselves with other influential educators to hold us accountable. When it comes to our areas of weakness, we are seeking out professional assistance in these areas, like we would a medical professional. And, once again, we are allowing other influential educators in our space that can coach and support us until those areas of weakness become oak strong.

Undoubtedly, we have grown to love many of the students we serve as our children or children in our families. But, claiming them as our own "children," "babies," or even "friends" requires more action from us than just lip service. Like our children, our students deserve educators who are genuinely willing to go above and beyond to ensure that they *always* receive the best lessons, resources, and opportunities. Our classrooms and schools have prepared them to approach the future with confidence. For students to get to this level of faith, it is going to require more doing on our ends but do not grow weary because, like our children, they are worth the ride.

## Classroom Strategies for Promoting Loyalty in the Classroom

**Create an Oath With Students (My Ten Point Program)**: When I think of an oath, I think of the Black Panther Party's Ten-Point Program. I think of what they demanded and promised to give to their communities. Being loyal to our students means that we not only support them wholeheartedly, but we also support their communities. And, we teach them how to do so as well. Using the BPP's Ten-Point Program is a great way to get to know what is vital to our students. It can also help them to develop a platform that outlines their values and core beliefs. When creating an oath with students, start by giving them a mini-lesson on the history of the Black Panther Party. Then, engage them in-class discussion about their 10-point program (yes, this can do this in any subject and any time during the school year). Follow-up the study by having students individually create their own Ten Point Program for their life and their education. Have students share their program with their peers and, as a class, create a classroom Ten Point Program that all teachers and students can agree to follow. You can extend this activity outside of the school by encouraging students to facilitate the creation of a Ten Point Program for the school. Their program will serve as an action plan as to how they can address problems in their communities through their program's vision and lessons learned in their classrooms. Once they have completed their action plan, they can use the problem-solution model to implement it. After the project, students can host a community meeting to update stakeholders on the nature of the project and its impact on the community.

**Say What?: Encyclopedia of Urban Slang:** I recently read of a sociology professor who maintained a spreadsheet with all of the slang words used by his students and what they meant. Keeping up with our students' lingo is a brilliant way to keep up with how it is changing. Creating an encyclopedia with students will also help us make sure we are enjoying students in the moment while preparing them for the future. Connecting with students and making every effort to understand the forces that influence them is an excellent way of demonstrating our loyalty to them. To incorporate the curation and application of language into our classrooms, have students create, organize, and maintain a digital encyclopedia of urban slang. For each word, have students note the word and create a definition of what it means. Also, they can include a visual representation or meme that depicts the word and a description of how this word can be used in or applied to a professional context or situation. Have students do this for every word and assign roles and responsibilities to students to ensure that the encyclopedia is kept up-to-date. At the beginning of a new school year, present the compilation to your new students and challenge them to keep the encyclopedia current throughout their school year.

**Bullet/Sketch Journaling:** Researchers say that one of the best ways to show loyalty to a person is through constant communication. Journaling is a great way to encourage continuous interaction between teachers and students. It can also serve as a way to check-in with our students and give them feedback and support. Allowing students the opportunity to reflect over their experiences, connect content with their realities, and plan for the future, can all be done through a bullet or sketch journaling. Journaling can be something that students do individually and then collaborate with classmates to bullet and sketch journal together. Using a digital tool in place of a journal might be tempting. But I encourage you to allow your students to put their pens to paper and go for it. Don't be ashamed to join the bullet journaling yourself.

**What's Your Hashtag/SLN (Student Learning Networks):** Using social media is a great way to connect with students. Through social media, we can also model how experiencing life through the lens of their peers is a way to build empathy for others that will, in turn, lead to loyalty. Also, social media is a great platform to encourage students to share ideas and support each other in bringing ideas to life or just working through a challenging problem. As educators, we are encouraged to join professional learning communities on social media as a way to grow professionally, so why not push our students to do the same? To start, challenge the class to create a classroom hashtag that will be used to post all things (appropriate) about the course. Their posts can include thoughts about something from class, questions they may have about an assignment, or epiphanies that finally hit them long after the class period was over. Student learning networks do not only have to be a space for academic purposes. SLNs can also be a space where students can have fun by collaborating with their peers. They can have cogenerative dialogues about their needs in the classroom, curate their work, or share it with the world. They can even post a selfie now and then to show the smile on their faces. What's your hashtag?

**Speak Their Love Language:** No relationship can work if you do not know the love language of the person that you are attempting to love. You can try to show them until you are blue in the face, but if you do not love them the way they need to be loved, then you take the risk of pushing them away. Like a relationship with a spouse, we must know and speak the love language of our students. The five love languages are: words of affirmation, acts of service, receiving gifts, quality time, and physical touch. A great place to start is by giving students a brief overview of the five love languages. Also, you can share your love language and give them examples of how they can speak to you in your love language. Follow this up with giving your students the Five Love Language assessment. The assessment can be coupled with a facilitated discussion to generate specific ways you can speak their love language in the classroom. Using love languages in our classes will ensure we are meeting our students' needs. Love languages can also help us love them in a manner that truly makes them feel welcomed.

SIX

# HELPING STUDENTS OVERCOME OBSTACLES THAT CREATE BARRIERS TO SUCCESS

*"As you grow older, you will discover that you have two hands, one for helping yourself, the other for helping others."*

MAYA ANGELOU

They say that if you can see it, you can achieve it. But can we? I think my 10th-grade year in high school was the time I grappled with this whole idea because the feeling of unworthiness blinded me. By then, I began to see and hear about many different things--college, career options, leaving Los Angeles, etc. But, all of that seemed as distanced as the Hollywood sign from South Central. It was hard for me to fathom the possibilities of my life when there were no tangible examples of those possibilities in my immediate sphere of influence. There was no one I could model my life after. And, every voice on the inside of me said that I was not good enough for a positive future. By the time I was 15 years old, my oldest brother was in prison. Again, my sister found her identity in stripping and prostituting. My mother was fresh out of jail and trying to adjust to life, and my best friend was expecting the arrival of her first child. My favorite cousin--Lamar--got killed after a fight at a house party, and my dad was struggling to provide for his new family. I had no real examples of what "success" looked like, and I couldn't envision ever "getting out" of Los Angeles, especially not to go to college. Why would I deserve anything different when I came from the same womb and the same home as them? None of my siblings had graduated from high school. So, my ability to see something different for my life was clouded. It did not help that I had little to no support on a journey that had so many different crossroads. I had one black friend in high school who had a parent who attended college, but that was it. I had my uncle, who was a student at the local junior college back in the 70s and 80s, but only earned his Associates Degree. The 10th grade is when I started to hear all of this talk about going to college, but what college would want me? I was barely passing my classes, and I skipped school whenever I felt like it. By fifteen, I found more excitement in finding other ways to cope with my trauma. No one checked on me or held me accountable to do or be more. So, I could not see more and honestly gave up on any desire that inspired me to want more. I mean, what made me think I should have more?

I settled for what my life would be by the time of my 16th birthday and became content with the thoughts of worthlessness. I was maintaining in school. But that was because I had found a social circle in the cheerleading squad. Cheerleading became an outlet to forget about my problems temporarily. However, that came to a halt when constant issues arose. It became too much to handle, so I found it easier to quit than to figure it out or better yet, to be figured out. It came to a point where I saw no value in anything I was doing because there was no value in me. Even when I tried doing good, what did it matter to someone destined to a future similar to my siblings? I thought if I surrounded myself with others who were trying to "do the right thing," then I could follow them. But, when the bell sounded at 3:00, we journeyed off to two different worlds. Many of them went to two-parent households or an environment where they had substantial support. I went home to figure many things out on my own and, when it got tough, I did what I knew how to do best and surrendered to the voices that teased me for having pipe dreams. The mountains became hard to climb, and the thought of climbing them made me feel like I was at the top of Mt. Everest--cold, alone, and running out of air. What was the point of me even continuing to try if I didn't know if I was on the correct path?

Whenever I stopped to ask for directions, I got them in a language that I could not comprehend. My friends had the support of the AVID (Advancement Via Individual Determination) program. But, when I tried to reach out to them for guidance and support, I was turned away because "you had to start the AVID program during middle school." I did not attend school in that district during middle school and was lying about my address in high school. So, I didn't even know programs like AVID existed. Once again, I tried, and it was a waste of time. I received a message that a better life was not for me. The tickets to board a train that would help me escape, well, those were passed out in middle school. The walls were caving in on me, and I could not get out. My anxiety increased at the simple thought of being trapped in South Central. So, guess what? I stopped caring. On the inside, I just gave up.

## But Do We Really Get It?

Dealing with trauma in the classroom is one of the biggest struggles for educators in urban schools. Some educators also battle with the concepts of sympathy versus empathy as a practice in their classrooms. Reaching out to care for a student who is haunted by past trauma or who is currently experiencing trauma is not easy to do. There are so many layers to a student who has experienced trauma. We must proceed with caution not to add to the pain that already exists. There is no such thing as a troubled kid. But, when we encounter children with extreme behavioral and emotional issues, we respond to them as if that is who they are. We do not consider the internal and external factors that wired their brains to act and react the way they do.

When I think of childhood trauma and the effects of trauma on one's identity, I think about the young and innocent faces of my siblings and

me. Recently, I had the pleasure of speaking with my preschool teacher--
Ms. Jones-- about what I was like as a child in school. The words she
used to describe me and my older brother, who was also a student of
hers, are words I will never forget. She described us as little "zombies"
who were always unhappy and unmotivated. We hated school but not
because of the work. School became an extension of the trauma we experienced at home. Because we were often sent to school dirty, hungry, and
unkept, we often became the target of our peers' laughs, jokes, and
discomfort. Ms. Jones even admitted that she "hated" being around us
because we smelt so bad and were *always* so dirty. By the time we
entered our adolescent years, we'd experienced neglect, foster care, isolation, racism, and sexual, and verbal abuse. We absorbed all of this while
watching our parents grow deeper and deeper into their alcohol and
drug addictions. We lived in a war zone where gunshots became a way
of life and could count on both hands how many close people we had
lost to senseless violence. We spent many nights traveling from crackhouse to crackhouse in search of our mother to find her unresponsive
with a pipe in her hand. We have seen our mother abused at the hands of
my father, abused by men on the streets, and run over by a moving
vehicle for owing drug money (well, this is how the story was told to us).
We've witnessed our mother arrested, homeless, and sleeping out of a
box on our front porch. We have seen her steal food and money from
right up under our noses. I would personally slide a mirror under the
bathroom door, sometimes, to see if she was getting high and then retreat
in tears. I have seen drug deals, the cooking of crack-cocaine, police
raids, and mental breakdowns where suicide was often contemplated.
After experiencing this, the next day, we got up, got dressed, and went to
school, holding all that had happened on the inside because no one
would understand.

I remember the several attempts made by well-meaning teachers to
console me with the words "I understand what you are going through,"
but did they? If they understood what I was going through on the inside,
why did they not act like it? I felt like I was not important enough for
them to stop what they were doing or teaching to respond to the genuine

needs that I had? If they understood, why did I not feel safe? Why was there no space in their classrooms to communicate what I was going through without fear of rejection or receiving a visit from child protective services? If they really "got it," then why was I struggling to keep up in their classes, with no support, and asked to leave their classrooms when I had one of my "acting out" episodes?

I entered schools and classrooms with so much shame from the trauma that I had experienced. Because of this trauma, I put up what scholar, researcher, and storyteller Berne Brown (2011) refers to as my "shame shield." According to Brown, in our classrooms, when students try to protect themselves from feeling bad, they use shame shields to defend themselves. There are three different types of shields that students, and people in general, wear. The "Moving Away" shame shield causes students to keep secrets and isolate themselves from others in fear of rejection. The "Moving In" shame shield leads to people-pleasing in fear of making others upset and being rejected. And, lastly, the "Moving Against" shame shield is used to combat hurt with hurt-- mostly trying to destroy someone emotionally before they are allowed to kill you. I sought to protect myself from all the trauma I packed on the inside. I wore whatever shield suited me best for the day. I entered school with my guard up, and if an emotional battle broke out, my shields were ready.

When students come into our rooms with their shields up, they cannot see us, and we cannot see them. As a result, learning cannot and will not happen. We must get students to take off their shields and let their guard down. Their guards come down when we create spaces that allow them to be vulnerable and protect and uplift them in their vulnerability. We reclaim our power by speaking about our shame, but we have to acknowledge that there is debilitating power in shame. When we allow this power in our classrooms, we create a space where shame dictates everything our students can be. To truly reach our students, we must provide opportunities for open conversations and guidance. Responsibly, we must support them to bring what shames them to the forefront confidently and safely. The shame of poverty, the shame of ethnicity, the shame of sexuality, the shame of culture, shame of religion--all that must be addressed and combatted in our learning spaces. We must challenge shame culture if we are going to help our students overcome the obstacles that hinder them from taking risks and dreaming BIG.

When I think about all the shame that I carried around, I think about the opportunity provided to me by my Algebra teacher, to release that shame and not become victim to it. See, letting go of shame is merely letting out all of those inner wounds that continue to make you feel bad and tell you that YOU.ARE.BAD. But, when they can no longer hide on the inside of you and make you fearful of the day someone would find out about them, you steal away the power of shame. Ms. Hyde gave me the tools that I needed--in the form of a journal--that allowed me to release the shame. She allowed me to be vulnerable with at least her when I was not ready to be vulnerable with anyone else.

Ms. Hyde met my vulnerability with pure empathy while walking alongside me in my mess. Through journaling and personal conversations, she helped me to realize that I was not the cause of anything that shamed me. For that reason, I had no reason to be burdened with guilt. She allowed me to see that the real power was in what I overcame, and despite all of the past trauma, I was still standing. She helped me turn my trauma stories into my testimony as I took the sting out of everything that once burned and caused me to hide in shame. When I stopped focusing on everything I was not, I began to open up and see everything I was. This new focus happened because I had a teacher who was patient and consistent enough to help me pull back the layers in a safe space. She got in the trenches with me and sought to feel my pain, no matter how uncomfortable it was. She got it, and she finally got me.

## Their Struggles Are Bigger Than Our Egos

Providing students a space to be vulnerable with us means that we have to take down our shame shields and be vulnerable with them. We cannot talk about being vulnerable if we are not willing to model vulnerability. How can we truly create a safe space for our students to open up if we are not comfortable in the very area that we are trying to create? As adults, we carry tons of shame around with us, and this shame dictates how we interact with our students and other professionals in our building. Because we have not dealt with our shame, we act in ways that are adverse to the learning environment that our students need to feel free. The famous saying goes: hurt people hurt people, and this does not change the moment we become certified educators. We carry this hurt into our schools and classrooms and release it in the form of bullying, name-calling, or public shaming of our students and colleagues. We issue it in the form of dishonesty, gossip, and backstabbing. Sadly, our students are watching and making notes about all they are witnessing. As a result, they internalize the belief that it is okay to become one with our "moving against" shields and use our pain and trauma to cause hurt and injury to others.

Professionally speaking, our classrooms are not therapy couches, and we should not look to students to act as trained therapists. However, we must model "letting go," if we are going to help them overcome. I remember being a third-year teacher who was on fire! I had great relationships with my students — solid friendships with my colleagues. And, stellar test scores to prove that we were working hard in the classroom. However, looking back, my ego caused me to create an environment that hindered my students in overcoming the obstacles that stood in their way. In the name of "keeping it real," I was quick to put students on the spot and shame them in front of their peers in the name of classroom management. I was a real jerk. I often distanced myself from students who I did not like because that was my way of guarding myself against the potential hurt from my students and protecting my ego. My classroom was not a place of love. My students had to walk on eggshells in fear of the responses they would get from me. I wasted tons of instructional time going toe-to-toe in heated word battles with students so they could not get the best of me. I refused to allow them to see me vulnerable because I was scared that any ammunition they had against me would be used to break me down.

The most vulnerable moment, and the most freeing moment, in my teaching career happened during a hallway conversation with a student. A student who was always smiling and respectful was giving me the "business" one day. He was wearing his *moving away* shield and quickly switched to his *moving against* shield when I continued to pick with him for shutting down and not working. His trauma had sent him into my classroom, ready for combat if provoked. My ego, coupled with my injury, caused me to pick a fight that I knew I had the upper hand in winning in the end. After kicking the student out of class (sounds familiar, right), I went looking for him. After I got off my ego trip, I just had to see what was wrong with him. After locating the student sitting in the hallway, I went to him, questioning what was wrong. In response, he replied, "nothing, I ain't been in the mood lately, and you are there tripping." I continued to probe, asking for him to explain what was causing him to "not be in the mood," and he continued to respond by saying, "you just wouldn't get it." By then, I had let my guard down and tried to show sympathy towards what he was experiencing internally. But, instead of fueling a connection, I was driving a disconnection with my words. I was telling him how awesome of a student he had been in my class and how great of a football player he was on the field. But, none of that was helping. As Berne Brown (2013) would say, in one of her many talks on empathy, I was looking down the hole he was in and trying my hardest not to fall in it with him. Despite the words that were coming out of my mouth, I was not providing him the outlet that he needed to be vulnerable with me or allow me into his heart. Even at that moment, I had my ego up. Although I was giving him bits and pieces of my story, I was only sharing the stuff that I assumed made me "real." I shared what it was like being from South Central and growing up in the hood, but I was not sharing the whole story. However, after a good fifteen minutes of going back and forth and probing, tears began to stream down the student's face. As I leaned in to comfort him, he became vulnerable even when I was not willing to do the same with him. "You don't get it," he said as tears continued to roll down his face. "You don't get what it's like to have a daddy as a crackhead!"

At that very moment, my spirit broke. Everything he thought I was not was everything I was. I knew very well what it was like to have a father who was once a crackhead. I currently had a mother who was addicted to crack. However, you would have never known that because of the show I put on and the secrets I kept. One of my biggest fears as an educator was my students finding out about my mom's drug addiction and imprisonment and throwing it up in my face. But, me holding on to my ego and my secrets was not serving my students when it came to helping them beat their odds. I became brave at that moment and broke my chains. I shared, with all of my students, the real me, and the battles that I fought dealing with parents who struggled with drug addictions. One of the things that caused me the most shame, I released by speaking about it. Allowing myself to connect on a deeper level, we both gained the courage that we needed to return to the classroom with our heads held high, and our shame shields down.

## Show Students How to Use What They Have to Get What They Want

Lack of vulnerability is a hindrance to all things we want our students to be. According to Brené Brown (2010), traits such as love, belonging, joy, courage, empathy, trust, innovation, creativity, accountability, hard conversations, feedback, problem-solving, and ethical decision-making all require vulnerability. We often view vulnerability as a sign of weakness, but it is the birthplace of our strength. It is an unfiltered ability to be who we are withholding any bars.

In our classrooms, and particularly those in urban schools, we must dispel the myth of what it means to be vulnerable. Many students in urban communities have become immune to their trauma. They believe that any show of emotion towards it is a sign of weakness. So, instead of unpacking all that makes them feel ashamed, they keep it in as a means to hold on to their pride. In many urban spaces, our youth turn to music, poetry, or other forms of artistic expression as a way of releasing their inner emotions. But, when they come into our schools and classrooms, there exist limited platforms for them to express themselves and receive unbiased support from their peers and educators while doing so. Again, educators have a responsibility to show our students that there is power in their vulnerability. And, we must create a space for them to actualize this power. Once students have realized the potential they possess, we must guide them in developing their strengths. They have to learn how to use their strengths to bring light to the trauma, such as racism, classism, sexism, homophobia, that exist in their communities.

So, how do we show our students how to use their trauma to overcome obstacles? I believe that the best way is to give our students space, freedom, and support to RELEASE and CREATE. We must remember the traits that stem from vulnerability. The students that we are seeking to prepare for future careers and opportunities must be courageous, empathetic, innovative, creative, and held accountable. As well, they have to be able to handle hard conversations, take positive and negative feedback, be efficient problem-solvers, and make ethical decisions in the best interest of others. I believe that many students from urban spaces already possess most, if not all, of these attributes. They don't know what to do with them. Students hide their strengths in fear of rejection. This fear is most common if rejection has happened in the past. The most prominent forms of trauma that exist inside the bodies of students in urban schools is the trauma of racism, poverty, and classism. And, we have not done a great job, as educators, in addressing and responding to the root causes of these various forms of trauma. As a result, students who are overcomers will not tap into their strengths in fear of being shamed and rejected once again.

To help our students bring out what is already inside of them, we must take away the threat of vulnerability in our classrooms and schools. How? Once again, by providing them with the space to RELEASE and CREATE. In this space, students have the opportunity to talk through their trauma or release their trauma through tools provided for them to create what's on their hearts. Some may think this sounds crazy. But I think one of the best places for this to happen is in the spaces we allot for in-school suspension or discipline. We already know that when a student is a challenge in class, removed from class, or caught skipping class, consistently, a more pressing issue is taking place on the inside. In response to this behavior, we typically give students an in-school suspension depending on the severity of the matter. We could start by changing the name of "in-school suspension" to something that removes the stigma like the "Student Support Center." Secondly, we can remodel the way the physical room appears to students and the vibe it sends. As well, we can change the person who monitors this room from a teacher serving out a mandatory duty to a professional educator trained in dealing with trauma. This professional educator should also have a track record of building solid relationships with students and providing quality instruction to all students. Get real; last thing students who are experiencing trauma on the inside need is to experience prison on the outside.

In our new "Student Support Center," students are provided flexible seating and access to various creative tools such as computers, coding equipment, art stations. They will also have access to traditional and digital tools, robotics equipment, studio recording equipment, and tons of pens and pencils for those who want to get it out on paper. During the intake process, students meet with school counselors or campus administrators who talk them through discussing the issues that might be troubling them. From this conversation, the administrator will pair the student with a campus mentor--someone who can follow-up and guide students through the release and creative process. Then, students are sent to a space to do something with their hands that will allow them to free their minds. After a student visits the "Student Support Center," they follow up with their assigned mentor. From their follow-up meetings, students have the opportunity to share what they created and receive feedback on their product. They will also get support in developing a plan of action that can be used to respond differently to situations that cause them to want to act out negatively.

A "Student Support Center" is a concept that can also happen in our classrooms. However, it cannot be associated with content instruction or discipline. Also, it cannot be a follow-up to shame and embarrassment distributed by the teacher. Before it can be useful in a classroom or any school setting, educators must do the work necessary. We must deal with our trauma but also deal with our biases that might cause a student to experience trauma while in our presence. After we have worked through our trauma on a personal and professional level, then we can create a safe space in our classrooms for students to release and create. Releasing and creating does not have to be in response to a behavioral situation or "acting out" episode. Remember, that the vision of a "Student Support Center" on our campuses is an alternative to handling discipline issues. However, we want to give ALL students space and opportunity to RELEASE and CREATE.

In our classrooms, the concept of releasing and creating should be a way of life. It should happen because our students need it, not because they've earned it. Ideally, it should happen at the beginning of class, where students are just allowed the space to decompress through creation and innovation. After students have been provided with the time and space to release and create, then they are offered the opportunity to be vulnerable and open. Allow them to share their final product and the significance of their project to the obstacles they are seeking to overcome. From here, teachers will follow-up with students, through conversation, to help them make sense of their frustrations turned into innovations. The goal of following up with students is also to guide them in understanding how they can utilize their skills in the future and turn their frustrations into productivity.

Suggesting giving students space and time to release and create or even making the proposal of using RELEASE and CREATE as a means of dealing with discipline may turn some educators off. However, GET OVER IT. Let's be real with ourselves. If our students are coming into our classrooms and schools with so much bottled up or spilling out, they are not ready to learn anyway. No matter how fun and engaging of a lesson you have planned, if their brains are too crowded to concentrate, then they will go through the motions. Or, they will disrupt students around them. We must be proactive. Going back to Chapter One--relationships take priority over the content and helping students deal with their trauma is a part of building solid relationships. We are not trying to "coddle" students or excuse constant misbehavior. Yet, we are taking charge by creating spaces where shame cannot survive. Here, trauma turns in triumph through hands-on support from empathetic educators who are ready to go to battle and get in the trenches with our students. We have to show students that they can turn life's messes into masterpieces. But first, they have to be vulnerable enough to pick up a brush and paint what's on the inside of them even if the world is not ready to see it.

## Classroom Strategies for Helping Students Process and Overcome Obstacles

**Code Switch On/Code Switch Off**: Language is a tremendous barrier to one's success. Especially when a country treats some languages as inferior. In urban communities, many of our students struggle in code-switching, which is alternating between languages in conversation. They find it difficult or are ashamed to use their home language and standard English interchangeably, and as a result, they develop an inferiority complex or remain silent. We must show our students the power of code-switching. How? By asking them to code-switch on and code switch off? What does this mean? Merely, it means that we provide students with space and opportunity to learn and know how to code-switch and when to code-switch. For example, after learning a new concept, ask students how they would explain and teach that concept to a family member, a close friend, their favorite musician, or a politician? They can demonstrate this through interactions with their peers or in writing. I prefer having students code-switch through scenarios and skits because code-switching is not only about what you say, but it is also about what you do. Something we, as educators, must model as well. To be clear, teaching students how to code-switch is not about changing who they are, and we must be careful not to come off that way. Do not use this as a means to shame or embarrass students. Instead, code-switching is about showing students that it is okay to use street jargon and professional language simultaneously. Code-switching is all about teaching students that they can be what professor Christopher Emdin (2018) refers to as

"Ractchedemic" or what political commentator Angela Rye (2017) calls "Sophistiratchet."

**Cultural Plunges:** We must show students that some challenges are not unique to specific groups, communities, and cultures when discussing the obstacles we face. What some cultures may view as an obstacle, other cultures may see as an opportunity to succeed. Cultural Plunges--activities that require students, outside of school, to spend time with someone from a different culture is an excellent way for students to learn about and appreciate the experience of others. It is also a unique way for our students to learn that some cultures have more in common than we think, one thing being the obstacles that we face in life. Encourage students to study another culture through a social outing, family gathering, or participation in a religious ceremony. Have them share the similarities and differences between the cultures. And, as it relates to overcoming obstacles, challenge students to explore the challenges that someone from another culture faces. Have them research the ways individuals, from various cultures, have mastered the barriers that stood in front of them and defied the odds. To conclude plunge activity, allow students to present what they learned about the individual, the community, and the culture from their interactions.

**Design Your Own School:** It is common to see numerous charter schools in urban communities. These schools exist because of someone's vision of changing the way teaching and learning is done in urban schools. They identified what they viewed as problems that were prevalent in the community and designed a model--or solution--to solving those problems. Ask your students if they had the opportunity to create a community school, what type of school would it be? What issues would this school attempt to address? How will the school serve its community? And, how would this school's curriculum shape students into community leaders and scholars? After you have thrown the question out there, step back and allow them the space to brainstorm and create. To take the challenge up a notch, review with your students what it takes to create a charter school in your state. Go over the steps--using your state's charter school application that it would take to make their charter school a reality. If you are brave, have your students go through the full process of designing their dream charter school. To do this, they will use the application and successful charter school models as their guide. Encourage students to submit their school design to the campus principal, school board, or even a representative from your state's education agency for review. From this experience, your students will learn a lot about what it takes to vision, design, create, and gain support for a model they believe will work. They will face many obstacles while designing their dream schools. But, through this productive struggle, they will learn how to create solutions to problems and overcome problems that hinder them from reaching their goals.

**Current Events = Teachable Moments:** How are you incorporating current events into your curriculum? If you do not, I encourage you to start ASAP! Using current events is a great way to help expose students to what is happening in their communities, state, country, and world. Also, current events create opportunities for teachers to engage their students in meaningful conversations about issues that might affect them. We can use these conversations as teachable moments in realistic ways to overcome obstacles. Current Events have been limited to primary schooling and social studies classes but should be present in all content levels in all areas. CNN Student News or CNN 10 are great resources to incorporate in class. But we should expose students to a variety of media forms, both in print and digital format, and different viewpoints when it comes to studying current events. Using current events in the classroom should not be done passively in the form of watch/read and write. We must be intentional about using current events to teach life lessons and helping students. We can accomplish this through meaningful reflective activities such as analysis of events, personal connections to events, and developing realistic solutions to problems they see others face.

**Problem-Solution Projects:** We are teaching a generation of students who face problems that we could not imagine. These problems exist outside of our schools and classrooms, but when they spill over into them, they affect what we do every day. Instead of ignoring these problems, we have a responsibility to help our students process the obstacles that stand in their way and develop realistic solutions to overcoming their obstacles. Problem-solution projects are a way for students to identify issues that affect their school and communities and develop meaningful solutions to solving those problems. However, students do not merely produce the solution and present on it. Yet, they collaborate with their peers to implement their solutions--through a school or community service project. After their project implementation, they create an action plan to follow-up with their project. As well, they continue advancing on what they once started with the betterment of the community in mind. The problem-solution model can apply to any content area. It is an effective way to provide students with integrated and extended learning opportunities while promoting independent problem-solving skills. Empowerment also comes from using the problem-solution project model because students see that with every challenge they face, there is something that they can do about it.

# SEVEN

# VISION FOR MY STUDENTS THAT GOES BEYOND WHAT THEY CAN SEE FOR THEMSELVES

*"We must believe that we are gifted for something and that this thing at whatever cost must be attained."*

MARIE CURIE

When Ms. Hyde gave me my first journal, it set me free. See, I was used to passing letters between friends and sharing my hopes and dreams with them, but I had never done anything like that with a teacher. I will always remember the moment she handed it to me wrapped all nice and neat. Inside the front cover was a little message of hope written just for me. It was something about this journal that still sticks with me today. Her giving me this journal was a turning point in my life. It was the moment when things started to make sense. I wrote in this journal as I had never written anything before. It was something about just letting what was on the inside of me out, and allowing someone who I had grown to admire read it, that made me see brighter days. For the first time in my life, someone was genuinely asking me to share my feelings. Importantly, she attempted to hold my hand and walk with me while I processed them. The journaling conversations between Ms. Hyde and me evolved into actual conversations.

She got to know me on a deeper level--all the fears, hurt, and pain--and I got to know her as well. While I began to see something different in her--someone who genuinely cared about what they were doing--she began to see something different in me. Her disposition toward me changed. With every conversation and interaction, she began to see less of who I was and more of what I could be with the right amount of support, encouragement, and guidance. And, she did not relent in seeing that I received the proper support, encouragement, and guidance while I was in school. The influence was so significant that it followed me out of school. I must say that there is a real power in teachers believing in students when students can't believe in themselves. Ms. Hyde, she put her money where her mouth was. Implementing an often overlooked component of culturally responsive teaching--caring--she saw, respected, and assisted me from my own "vantage point" and helped me grow "academically, culturally, and psycho-emotionally." She did not impose her desires on me, nor did she assume an absence of capability or responsibility. Instead, she believed in me, identified my assets, and leveraged them in her teaching in a responsive and relevant way. In essence, her "caring for" me assisted me in blossoming into a better student and, honestly, human being (Gay 2018, p. 58).

She did not only show me that she saw something more significant in me through her words, but she also proved how invested she was in me through her actions. In every way possible, she set me up for success. She encouraged me to surround myself with others--through clubs, organizations, and extracurricular activities--who would bring out of me what she saw in me. She knew that if she did not have the power or the resources to do what was needed, she found someone, or something, that could. By the time I was in my junior year of high school, I had a well-established support system of teachers and other campus officials. A few of these educators were strangers who willfully invested in me. Having this team of teachers and educators looking out for me, gave me a new perspective on what my life could be and proverb "it takes a village to raise a child." The whole village (the entire school) stepped up and stepped in as the result of a teacher who did not cancel me out. Because she saw greater in me, I saw greater in myself and began to shine a light that allowed others to see me from the inside out. I had a new confidence about myself that all stemmed from someone providing me a safe space to be vulnerable. Someone who put systems in place that ensured if I had fallen, while in school, someone was going to pick me up, dust me off, and support me in trying again.

I had some support at home with my grandmother and uncles. But I had never known what it felt like to have a team of people around you, cheering and pushing you on. And boy, I had a team. Made up of teachers, administrators, counselors, and coaches, this team had my back. They pushed me to the point that I had no other choice but to fight for something different and better than my norm. It was too many people cheering for me and counting on me for me to give up again. The power of positive reinforcement left me with no option but to shine. My team told and showed me that everything that I was not was all that I needed to become who they knew I could be.

## When We Can See It, Help Them Believe It and Achieve It

Having one teacher who believed in me and acted on her beliefs was all that was needed for me and others to see what I had the potential to achieve and become. Her confidence in me inspired others to see something different in me that they may not have seen before. As a result of this belief, I now had a team of educators who took me in. They set high standards for me and held me accountable for reaching and maintaining them. This took some time, setbacks, and hard conversations. I was the least bit coddled, and when I did decide to go against the grain, in all love, they allowed me to experience the natural consequences of my actions. But they never gave up on me. My team was reliable and would not let me go down without putting up a fight. When I was tempted to do something wrong, I self-corrected because I did not want to disappoint them. I refer to this group of educators as a "team," because when it came to me, they were just that.

If you think about the qualities of any good team--like the Golden State Warriors-- they are not going after the same things in isolation of one another. They are not wearing the same jerseys and chasing after the same ball with five different goals in mind. Yet, while on the court, they have one goal and must work together to accomplish this one goal. What makes this team effective is their ability to work together to be a winning team, indeed. They might bring in specialists to consult them in getting better at the game of basketball. But all the work is done by them with the leadership of their coach. This leadership is essential to the success their team has had over the years. Dominating the game of basketball, with several championship titles under their belt, did not just happen because they all showed up to work and did their things. But their success is a result of constant practice and team development. A player added to the team joins with confidence, knowing that they are entering a group of men who truly understand the concept of a team. They under-stand how all of their different roles and responsibilities, combined, win games and increase their probability of winning an NBA Championship title. What I admire about the Warriors is how in sync they are with one another. They effectively communicate sometimes without communi-cating at all. They have one goal in mind, and everyone plays their part. While on the court, they continuously fight to win despite what the scoreboard says. Overall, they stay in the moment, encourage one another, and have fun while on and off the court. They have a reliable team, and because of this, the vision of being successful is easy to see, while others continue to question what makes them one of the top teams in the NBA.

How many of our students can say that they have a "solid" team of educators who are looking out for them and pushing them to be great? Not just one teacher or an administrator, but an actual group who is strategic about ensuring that all students are successful? Sadly, not many. Most students have those one or two teachers who they can count on for the nudge. However, it takes more than one or two teachers to push students out of their comfort zones and pull them up to greatness. Students in urban schools have a better chance of being successful when they have a community of people surrounding them with safeguards. Because one's community--or village--shapes how we view the world, the community also plays a vital role in how we see the possibilities of the world.

The team I had in high school had all been places and done things that I imagined doing in life but did not know where to start when it came to making it my reality. Because they collectively saw potential in me, they worked together to place me in clubs and organizations that I would thrive in and achieve what was once unattainable to me. They observed that I was an outspoken and creative visionary who was not afraid to step up and take a leadership role, and they invested in that. By the end of my junior year of high school, I made tremendous strides because of the investment my team made into my life. I was in student council, a member of the Black Student Union, and had even won a Lion's Club Speech Contest at the local and district level. My successes were possible because my team saw what I viewed as nothing and made it into something. They exposed me to professions that would shape me into the educator, historian, author, and entrepreneur that I am today.

The way my team invested in me is the way teams like the Brooklyn Nets invested in player Kevin Durant after what some called a lousy season. While starting for the Golden State Warriors, during the 2019 NBA season, Kevin Durant sprained his calf, which kept him on the bench up until game 5 of the NBA finals. Durant made a stellar return starting in game 5. However, about 20 minutes into the game, he had suffered yet another injury--this time, it was a ruptured Achilles. Many speculated that this would ruin the 2020 NBA season for Durant and the Warriors. However, the nation was shocked when, on June 20, 2019, he announced that he was leaving the Golden State Warriors and would be joining the Brooklyn Nets. Yes, even after suffering a setback of an injury, he was still of value.

Kevin Durant, being picked up by the Nets, is the perfect example of helping our students believe and achieve what they cannot see. He was at his lowest and suffering an injury that would be hard to recover from, but a team was still willing to recruit him and add him to their roster. The Nets did not see what Durant was lacking but saw everything that was beneath the hurt and pain of his injury. Since the start of his career, he has proven himself as a player consistently. The Nets knew what Durant was capable of doing and the potential successes he could bring to their team. Because of the potential they saw, they were willing to invest in him returning to the court as the star player they knew he could be. To make sure that he returned as his best, they surrounded him with their best to ensure that he made full progress in his recovery. They saw the potential, so they invested in the potential. They picked him up and set him up when he probably did not even know where to start when it came to getting back up.

When we see students struggling in our schools, we must not be quick to throw them to the wayside or give up on them when they refuse to give into us. Like Kevin Durant was to the Brooklyn Nets, we must see beyond the injuries and invest in them. We must put a reliable team around them at all costs, especially when we can sense what they are capable of accomplishing. We see students in our buildings roaming with no hope, motivation, inspiration, or ambition. We must help bring out their hidden potential no matter the cost. All of our students have faith inside them. We have to help them remove the layers of debris that is covering it up. It may not be easy and may not happen overnight, but it can happen if we are strategic and patient about it happening. A big part of helping students achieve what they can't see is exposing them to what they have never seen. In our schools and classrooms, that means we are exposing them to different possibilities of life and showing them how that possibility can become their reality. It is also imperative to place them in environments surrounded by a diverse group of like-minded-people pursuing similar dreams and visions.

When changing students' settings, do not seek to change them or their realities. Instead, guide them in building a solid action plan that will help them transform their realities. Support them as they began to act on and live out what was once unimaginable. A reliable team MUST first be put in place before you take a student out of their comfort zone. Our students must know that there is a force higher than them backing them up, pushing them forward, and cheering them on to greatness. Our schools must start the initiative in helping students defy the odds. The school must become that reliable team. No matter how challenging the call is, students must see that they exist in a school-community that sees the potential in them and will help them fight to maximize that potential.

## Gardens Can Grow in The Ghetto

I am a self-proclaimed TED Talk addict. I find real joy in viewing TED Talks and the ideas shared by brave souls and experts in their professions. Most importantly, I love to see others putting themselves out there and sharing their dreams with the rest of the world. Recently, I came across a TED Talk titled "A Guerilla Gardener from South Central." Being that I am a native and lover of South Central, Los Angeles, I automatically clicked play. Listening to Ron Finely share his passion for bringing fresh food to his community--via planting gardens on sidewalks owned by the city--gave me hope. He shared how the garden outside his very own home became not only a place of inspiration in the community but a place that also feeds and serves the community. Finely's garden gave hope to many in a city that was "home of [the] drive-thrus and drive-bys."

See, growing up in South Central, Los Angeles, I had never seen a garden before, especially not walking down the streets of my neighborhood. I never knew that gardens could grow in the ghetto. But, after actually seeing one blossoming on the curbside, full of delightful veggies, I saw my own "hood" from a new perspective. What was once a cold, dark, and violent place masked by the golden California sun was a place of beauty and hope. Ron's gardens evolved into something that became more than just a site that provided the community with access to fresh foods. It became a tool for education, jobs, community service, sustainability, and a step in the right direction of changing the perception of South Central. See, what Ron did was not only plant gardens in his community, he transformed his neighborhood by "changing the composition of the soil." The people became soil. From planting the right seeds in that soil--seeds of hope, seeds of empowerment, seeds of innovation, seeds of self-sustaining--people in the community of South Central began to take back their neighborhoods. They did this, slowly, joining Ron in planting gardens, choosing fresh food over fast food, and picking up shovels instead of picking up guns. If we want to see a change in the community, we must be intentional about changing the composition of the soil.

Schools in urban communities have become gardens with weak soil composition. Nothing is growing from it because it only gets the basics, occasionally. However, there is still this expectation that one day, it will become fruitful, over time, and begin to produce. What I have witnessed in urban schools is similar to the dry, brittle, and ugly parkway that once existed outside of Ron Finely's house. It was a public space where grass grew sparsely. It served its purpose of separating the sidewalk from the traffic on the street. However, apart from that, the parkway served no real benefit to the community. Occasionally, people who traveled by foot found it useful. However, the parkway served no purpose to the masse in a city overpopulated with motorized vehicles and public transportation. It was practically useless when it came to meeting the real needs of the community.

Sit and ponder on this question: what is your school or your classroom doing to meet the real needs of the community? Most of our schools and classrooms are doing nothing to meet the needs of the city. While we service kids from the community, we do not see the true potential in the community. In our schools--our gardens--we are not intentional about changing the composition of the soil that has the potential to change the city. No change is happening because we do not believe that gardens can grow and sustain in the ghetto. So, as a result, we stick to the same old same old when it comes to the way we do teaching and learning in urban schools. We don't reconsider our pedagogy and practices because we have predetermined the potential of the soil based on past produce.

The problems that exist in urban communities is a direct reflection of the issues that exist in urban schools--not vice versa. Again, if we want to change urban communities, we have to change the soil in urban schools. As educators, we are the gardeners, and our students are the soil. Like the soil, we should see them as what Ron Finely refers to as "blank canvas" with so much potential. However, we only realize this potential if we are conscious and intentional about tending to and transforming the soil as a means of bringing beauty and restoration to our communities and schools. Our gardens should become places of inspiration, hope, and endless possibilities from the effort and work educators/gardeners have put into turning a blank canvas into a work of art.

A garden turned into a real work of art is not a by-product of the basics. Instead, it is the manifestation of the gardener's vision, time, and sacrifice to bring the best out of something that others wrote off as invaluable and useless. It became a vision actualized by someone who saw beyond what was in front of them. So, how do we change the composition of the soil in our schools to improve the community? Like Ron Finely, we identify the problems that are causing the land to lack nutrition, and we develop intentional solutions to transforming its composition. We move from focusing on test prep and test scores and focus on the skills that will create future local and global leaders. To do this, in our classrooms, we support students in identifying problems that exist in their communities and show them that within them lies the solution to solving those problems. We show them the beauty of their communities by getting them out in their communities as agents of change. We cultivate them into critical thinkers fueled with empathy and global stewardship. We show them through hands-on community-based lessons what their neighborhoods can transform into if they are conscientious about taking them back. We show them that gardens can grow in the ghetto, but educators must be the ones who lead the initiative of tilling the soil and planting the seeds. We change students' perception of learning and prepare and inspire them to be more and watch the community buy-in and transform in response.

## Discovering Their Purpose

Upon entering my home, the first thing you will see are smiling faces. What started as one smiling face has grown into hundreds of smiling faces. There are so many smiling faces on this windowsill turned into a picture frame that I often have to rotate and switch these smiles in and out. And every year, the smiling faces grow in numbers. When visitors come into my home, I am so excited that the very first thing they will see is these smiling faces. These faces, which I can still point back to the first day I met each one of them, are not the faces and smiles of close family members and friends. But these are the faces and smiles of former students who became like family and friends.

What I love most about my wall of fame is looking at each face and remembering their stories. My heart warms with pride that at the moment that they needed me the most--those tough last two years of high school--I was able to be there and be a part of their team. I think back to who many of them were when they sat in my class. I jump for joy at the path they are on now. From what rapper Khalid called "young, dumb, and broke high school kids" to college graduates, doctors, lawyers, educators, mentors, community organizers, great parents, and husband and wives, my heart is warmed at seeing my "babies" step into what they once thought was far out of reach. Everyone has a divine purpose in life. While some come out of the womb knowing what their purpose is, others take years and sometimes many trial and errors to discover it. Despite the path that they journey down to find out who they are, we must travel with them and help them find out all the options that await them. Some may believe that the path to discovering one's purpose in life is out of our hands as educators. Believe it or not, we possess more power than we know when it comes to students discovering what they are truly meant to do in life.

Earlier in this chapter, I discussed creating what Brené Brown (2017) refers to as "Daring Classrooms," where students can be who they indeed are without fear of shame. When it comes to discovering our purpose, shame holds us back because we are afraid to disappoint others with what truly makes us happy in life. Life coaches and purpose experts will tell you the primary indicator of finding and being in your purpose is doing what makes us happy each day. We must do something that is not about the money but about the joy and gratification that we feel when doing it. To get this across to students, we have to help them discover what truly brings them pleasure and satisfaction. We do this by giving them space to be and do what makes their hearts feel at peace.

Students discovering what "feels right" and their genuine passion will not happen if we do not instill in them the root of living a purpose-driven life. Experiencing this life requires risk-taking and acceptance of failure. We are preparing a generation of students who have taken the saying "failure is not an option" to heart but far out of its original context. As a result, they will not travel into uncharted territory out of fear of failure. "Failure is not an option" does not mean staying where you know there is a risk of failing. It means to go into the unknown, and if you fail, get back up and try again. Students are uncomfortable with taking risks--especially in the classroom--if they cannot assess the potential outcome beforehand. They echo "you only live once (YOLO)," but are living in" fear of missing out" (FOMO) and not pleasing others' lifestyles. WE have to get them past this if we want to influence their steps in discovering their real purpose in life.

The lingering questions now are: how? How do we help students discover their purpose? First, we move away from the belief that there exists only one way to solve a problem or that every lesson will come with a rubric or exemplar. Why are we reinforcing "people-pleasing" and "this is what it should look like" when we know that that is not the way life works out. We did not discover our life's purpose by checklists or someone else's standard of perfection. We instead pursued what we loved and did that. Taking risks was a part of our journey, but we get into our classrooms and force our students to stick to the script. Risk-taking should be an everyday thing in our class for our students while we gently follow behind to let them know they have our support. We take away the rubrics and exemplars and allow our students freedom in learning. We take them off this meaningless path to nowhere, which results in high levels of anxiety and unsafe practices of coping. Instead, we provide them with space where it is okay to fail. If they gave it their all, did what worked for them, are willing to accept feedback, then we help them get back up and start over.

Secondly, discovering purpose in life means we have to show students how to put all of their cards on the table. Putting themselves out there, confidently, can only be done when we allow them to be vulnerable in our spaces. Our students come to our rooms with a sense of what makes them happy, and they can do effortlessly. However, they have a fear of putting it out in the open. Or, they have suppressed their life's desires because we have sent the wrong messages of what success is and what success is not. We put the doctors, attorneys, scientists, and tech innova-tors on pedestals, when it comes to ideal careers, and reduce the artists, musicians, designers, models, creatives, and influencers down to side hustle. We tell our students that they must be "go-getters" if they are going to make something out of their lives. But we then discouraged them from going after what they want out of life and teaching them how to play it safe.

Helen Keller once said that "avoiding danger is no safer in the long run than outright exposure. The fearful are caught as often as the bold." Knowing this to be accurate, why do we discourage the process of taking a risk when our students can still fail at playing it safe? They can look at rubrics and exemplars all day long and again turn in something that does not meet standards. They can get into all the top colleges in the world and fail under pressure. They can go after that high paying career and make someone else millions of dollars. Then, fall into a state of depression because they have chosen to do what makes others happy or what would pay the bills and not what they were created to do.

We have to expose students to the consequences of being bold and what can come from their pursuit of happiness. In doing so, we have to let them know that failure is a possibility but something they can learn from and overcome. They can discover new meanings in life by failing at what they thought their lives should be. They must leave our classrooms and schools knowing that they all possess a purpose in life, and there is no one right way to discover that purpose. The learning environments that we create must become danger zones. However, the danger must be in what lies ahead if students do not take that risk or that first step on the path to the unknown. We must show and remind students that their real purpose in life is being themselves. Not a carbon copy of someone else. We must evaluate students and hold them accountable to do what only they can and were created to do. With every opportunity we present to them to learn and demonstrate something new, we must judge them off of their capabilities and passions and not the abilities of others. Albert Einstein's once said, "Everybody is a genius, but if you judge a fish by its ability to climb a tree, it will live its whole life believing that it's stupid." We must remember this quote if we are going to help students discover their purpose genuinely. Our students need to know that it is okay to "do you boo-boo." It's okay to make a profession and a life out of doing what makes them happy. They can live life doing what they enjoy while bringing joy, inspiration, and change to the lives of others.

## Classroom Strategies for Sharing Your Vision with Students and Helping Them Create Their Own

**Vision Board Party**: Over the past couple of years, vision boards have become a popular way of planning and creating an action plan for the life we dream of living. Vision boarding can be used and connected to any content area. While it is a great tool to use in general terms of life planning, it is also a great tool to use in career explorations. Helping students create a vision for their lives, also means exposing students to all the options of life. Each content area should incorporate into its curriculum a focus on career options related to the discipline. Students should know the career option by name. They should also understand what is required to make it to that career, thrive in that career, and what the outcomes of life could be if they pursued that career. No matter what subject or grade-level you teach, have your students put together a vision board no matter if it is personal or content-specific. The first step in actualizing the future is realizing what lies ahead in the future.

**1 Minute of Gratitude**: Counting our blessings and being thankful for what we have at the moment is crucial to visioneering. Many students struggle with visioning the future because they see no real value in where they are or what they have in the now. To help them move past this, we have to show them how to appreciate even the smallest things in life. We must provide them with the space to exercise gratitude even when they feel they have no reason to be thankful. Allow students to keep a journal. Because our bodies become immune to positivity when it is overdone, 2-3 times a week, allow your students time to write, reflect, and express their thankfulness. This activity is personal to them. While we are to guide them in appreciating even the smallest things in life, it is not our place to judge them on how they express gratitude. Students can journal in a traditional format, digital format, through blogging or vlog-ging. Allow it to start as something personal then move students in the direction of sharing their gratitude with the classroom and eventually a global audience. With gratitude comes a change of attitude, and, for our students, practicing 1 minute of gratitude throughout the week can put them one step closer to finding true happiness in life.

**Genius Hour:** In their 2014 IPO, Google founders encouraged their employees to spend 20% of their time working on something they believed would benefit Google. The goal was to empower their employees to be more innovative and creative, on Google's time, while still working for the greater good of the company. Many educators have attempted to implement the 20% time concept, genius hours, or passion projects, into their classroom. This time is to allow students to explore what interests them and create something meaningful in the process. I am all for 20% time, genius hours, and passions project. I love giving students the freedom to dream of the future and create. However, when having our students create, we cannot allow them to stop there and not move on. We must guide them in the doing and following through with their creations for this concept to truly work in our classrooms. Help students discover their purpose in life and also help them determine how to use their gifts as a means to global stewardship. They can talk about and present their awesome ideas all day long, but if it stops there, then the concept is ineffective. Do the 20% time, genius hours, and passion projects.

Give them a shot in your classrooms by challenging students to envision and create something that will be realistic and related to your content area and has the potential to benefit your school and their communities. However, follow-through by showing students how to implement what they have created in their schools and neighborhood. Teach them about trial and error. Let them see that their ideas may not produce the results they imagine, but it's okay to go back to the drawing board and readjust. Gmail was one result of Google's 20% time, but that did not happen by just talking to others about it. Gmail had to be brought to life, tested by others, put out into the world, and updated to meet the needs of the people. Imagine the growth we will see in our students if we get them out in their schools and communities, bringing their thoughts and ideas to life.

**Dear Younger Me/Older Me Janus:** We get the month of January from the Roman god Janus who was believed to always look backward in the past and forward to the future. To help students create a vision for themselves, have them draw a Janus that reflects on their history and envisions the possibilities of the future--one life with two different meanings. To make this activity engaging, have students create an outline of their bodies on butcher paper. Then, decorate their bodies where one side is looking back, and the other side is looking forward to the future they want for themselves. Janus bodies are also a great tool to promote critical thinking in our content areas. It can be used to compare and contrast historical figures or movements in history, analyze character development in social studies, compare hypotheses in sciences, and discover the best steps in solving an equation in math. Janus represents the past and the future occurring at the same time. He is also a doorway to pushing students out of comfort zones to see what lies ahead

**Student Influencers:** Being an influencer is becoming a booming profession, especially among millennials and students of Generation Z. Influencers are helping us decide, and frequently, dictating what we eat, what we wear, what we listen to, and even how we structure our day. If being a professional influencer is evolving into one of the many career options for the future, we must prepare our students to step into this role. How? We help guide them in using social media platforms--Facebook, Twitter, Snap Chat, and Instagram--to start influencing the decisions that their peers are making. In doing so, we begin by creating a dialogue about what issues, in our schools and communities mainly, are essential to students. Once we understand those issues, we support students in developing a responsible social media presence. We guide them in the ways they can use their voices and talents to help others make what can seem like a challenging decision. We help them in safely sharing their thoughts, ideas, and promotions. We engage them in follow up conversations on how developing as an influencer can help prepare themselves and others for the future. With all things, we also encourage them to connect to content, so they see the big picture behind what's in the classroom. We must also teach them how to conduct necessary and appropriate research before they put anything out on a global platform. Being an influencer is a profession that I do not see fading away. We have to prepare students to step into this role as a means of educating them for the future.

# EIGHT

# EDUCATE THEM ACCORDING TO WHAT THEY CAN BE AND NOT WHAT YOU CURRENTLY SEE

*"Education is the passport to the future, for tomorrow belongs to those who prepare for it today."*

MALCOLM X

In 2004, my grandmother took a trip to Las Vegas, which was her getaway spot. When she returned to Los Angeles, she would not stop talking about a man she had met on a bus who worked for the admissions office at Grambling State University. My grandmother was born in Pioneer, Louisiana. So, with Grambling being the premier Historically Black College and University in Northeast, Louisiana, it was near and dear to her heart. What she loved most about Grambling was its World Famed Tiger Marching Band. Because I was one of her only grandchildren on the right track, Grambling became her dream school for me to attend. By 2004, I was ready to get out of high school, but I had no big plans.

My friends were applying to all of the University of California colleges or Cal State colleges. Yet, I found contentment with the minimum wage job I had at a local grocery store and possibly taking a few classes at the local community college. By my senior year of high school, I was making better decisions, and my grades were decent. But I did not believe my low GPA would get me into any of the local Cal State Colleges. I was not cut out for any of the schools in the UC System. Plus, I was in what I thought was a serious relationship and convinced myself that I was getting married once I had officially turned eighteen. But my grand-mother would not stop with this talk about Grambling State University and how I just had to go and check it out. She gave me the contact infor-mation of the admission counselor she met on her trip. Because I did not want to disappoint her, I reached out and gave him a call. Although I had reached out, I had no intention of going to Grambling. I made contact with him to get my grandma off my back. This contact was also a smokescreen for my peers. I wanted them to believe I, too, had intended to go to college after high school.

During my conversation with Mr. Osborn, despite my lack of enthusiasm and low GPA, he encouraged me to submit an application and register to attend the upcoming freshman orientation. He said I should go to Louisiana and check Grambling out. If I did not like the school, then I did not have to attend. The following day, I went to my school's Student Resource Center to inquire about my possibilities of going to Grambling. Both my oldest sister and brother did not graduate from high school, which was very disappointing to my grandmother. I did not want to be another disappointment to her after all she had sacrificed for me growing up. I did not have access to the internet or computer at home. So, my school's college advisor, Ms. Parson, helped me research Grambling and apply for admission. My grandmother and my uncle were willing to cover the cost of me going to the freshman orientation. I met some other people from my neighborhood who were going as well, so I figured what did I have to lose. I had never been out of Los Angeles unsupervised, and I was going to spend a week on a college campus with no adult supervision. I never promised anyone I was going to return to Grambling, so it was a win-win situation from me. After my trip, I could return home and tell her I did not like it. I would enroll for a few basic classes at the local community college and get married to my boyfriend like I had planned to do.

I jumped off the Greyhound bus in Grambling, Louisiana--the most "countriest" city I had ever seen. It felt like the temperature was one million-degrees. After previewing the town, I told myself there was no way I was returning to this country place. I was a city girl, and there was no way I was going to survive being in the middle of nowhere. But, since I was there for the weekend, and looking to have a good time, I put those thoughts aside, grabbed my bags from the bottom of the bus, and made my way to check-in. After I was successfully checked-in, I hunted down Mr. Osborne, who had a Student Ambassador show me my room and where I would be staying for the week. When I got to my room, my roommate had already checked-in, unpacked, and was out with her family. I unpacked, made up my bed, and sat and stared at the wall, trying to contain my emotions of feeling lonely and afraid. It was emotional because I had never been outside of Los Angeles (unless it was on a weekend trip to Vegas). Also, I had never been away from my grandmother or Uncle Benny for more than a weekend. I did not like the feeling, and I did not like Grambling.

My roommate finally made it to the room right before it was time to go to the dining hall--or the Cafe--and the first event scheduled for orientation. My first encounter with her was very transformative. She was from Baltimore, Maryland, and came from a middle-upper class black family. Her mom was a Grambling Alumni who was now a high school principal in Baltimore. What shocked me about my roommate was that her upbringing and disposition were opposite of mine. Coming from South Central, I had never met middle-upper class blacks who had a family legacy of being college-educated. It was something about her that made me feel uncomfortable but intrigued at the same time. This week exposed me to a whole new world. I was in a sea of people who looked like me, came from places like me, and had similar stories like mine. The only difference was they were not content with their condition and wanted more for their lives after high school and after college. I witnessed African Americans from all across the United States--some were even from Los Angeles, who were lawyers, doctors, educators, and politicians. They had excelled in their careers. Now they were seeking to inspire high schoolers who wanted to become lawyers, doctors, educators, and politicians in a place whose motto was "Everybody Is Somebody." During orientation week, I met people whom I had fallen in love with and some who inspired me. I wanted more. I did not know what I was going to do with myself when I returned to Grambling, but I had to return. Deep down inside, I knew I was somebody. During my time on Grambling's campus, I encountered countless other young African Americans who, too, knew they were somebody. We were all looking to become more. Grambling was the place to be, and there was no way I was not going to be in that place come the Fall of 2004.

## The Power of High Expectations for ALL Students

Before leaving Grambling, I met and exchanged contact information with many people who vowed to hold me accountable for returning to Grambling. They offered me whatever support I needed to gain acceptance for the upcoming school year. When I returned to California, my grandmother's and uncle's hearts were pleased to know that I had genuine intentions on attending Grambling in the Fall. However, the road to getting accepted to Grambling would not be an easy one. I had to take the ACT and secure financial aid to attend college. I also had to graduate from high school. Graduating from high school meant I had to reshift my focus. Life could no longer revolve around working and chasing my boyfriend, whom I believed that I would one day marry. My team of educators was elated to hear that I had decided to give Grambling a shot. They also vowed to hold me accountable to get there.

However, that accountability came with a cost. Each of them increased the bar when it came to what they expected of me and rode my butt to ensure that I did not fall off track or get distracted. I had teachers in the classroom refusing to relent and administrators out on the yard, ready to get me back in check if necessary. I had Ms. Parson in the Student Resource Center, making sure I was signed up and studying for the ACT. She was always on my case about submitting my FAFSA and sending transcripts to Grambling. I had Mr. Osborn always calling my grandmother and me to make sure I was still coming to Grambling. My uncle was becoming more aggressive in checking my grades and making sure I was submitting all assignments and passing my classes. All around me, someone was riding my back. The pressure, encouragement, support, and belief that I could accomplish something pushed me to grind harder than I had ever grind before.

See, there is real power in setting high expectations for students and holding them accountable in ensuring that they meet those expectations. High expectations send the message to students that we know there is greatness within them and will not let up until that greatness comes out of them. Based on the data that exist from studies conducted on high expectations in low performing minority schools, clearly defined high expectations yield positive results. Consistent high expectations create students who will produce results. Put them up to the test, and these students will prove themselves in all cases. Unfortunately, low expectations for students from urban spaces is the problem with urban schools. Many campuses have an inspiring mission statement and mottos, but they do not hold to that mission, nor do they require their teachers to do so. When the bell rings and doors close, students with so much potential are handed the short end of the stick as a result of someone's deficit thinking or pity.

Students in urban schools possess more potential than you know, and can compete with the best when adequately prepared to do so. But that preparation starts with us as educators, not their homes or their communities. Having high expectations goes well beyond telling students what we think they can achieve. High expectations mean high-quality curriculum and instruction. It requires us to get off our butts and provide top-notch instruction and learning opportunities for students. Learning becomes intensive and will take students out of their comfort zones, making them sweat mentally and physically. Having high expectations means that when a student fails at something, we do not reduce the rigor or move-on. We go back to the drawing board, consider differentiated ways to show mastery, place the task back in their hands, and have them go for it again. We do not allow any students to find contentment in what they can't do. Yet, we scaffold, guide, and cheer them on until they see for themselves what they can do. Urban students do not need a savior. They need educators who are willing to break down barriers that hinder their access to resources and opportunities and do the work necessary to provide them with an education that will set them up for success.

I have seen and heard of far too many times when children of color were robbed of quality education because of lazy and inept educators--not lazy and incompetent students. This issue has often left me questioning where the real deficit lies--in the abilities of the teacher or the skills of the student. Having and acting on high expectations comes at a cost for us educators. To require high expectations from our students, we have to first address the reasons behind our beliefs that some students can succeed while other students can't. Secondly, we must consider our definition of success and what limitations it places on students, and we must increase the bar when it comes to the way we approach instruction in classrooms. You cannot be a lazy teacher and have high expectations at the same time. High expectations will require you to also step out of your comfort zone. It means that you will have to keep up with changes in education, refresh your pedagogy, and attend professional developments to help you grow. For some, you will finally have to get from behind your desk or podium and get in the trenches. High expectations are more than just assigning difficult problems or giving countless meaningless projects and tasks. To truly set high expectations for your students, it requires self-regulation and self-reflection. You have to prepare yourself to do things differently, especially if we expect our students to do things differently.

I laugh when I hear teachers talk about what their students cannot handle because of factors outside of their control. I also take it personally because I was one of those students who once had low expectations set for them. In response to hearing a teacher say what a student cannot do, I follow-up with the questions: Is it that they cannot do it? Are they not doing it in a way suitable for you? Have they told you they can't do it? Or, have you assumed they cannot do it?" My final question is the one that always stops an educator in their tracks. Would you be okay with your child's teacher telling you that something was too high-level for your child, so they did not give them a shot at it? We have to stop under-estimating the potential of students who come from urban communities. They know and can do more than what we think they can — it's all about the mind and what we feed to it. If we feed our brains low standards and expectations, then that is what it will produce. Especially when that's all it's told it was capable of doing.

For many years, I taught a Dual Credit and Advanced Placement United States History course in an urban school district. It took me some time, and frustration, to adapt to the nature of the test to teach the skills neces-sary. I eventually decided to stop focusing on the test altogether, espe-cially knowing that many standardized tests are inequitable and not designed with relevant opportunities for all students to demonstrate academic abilities. Students knew they would be expected to take the test but were confused as to why we "never focused on the test" and testing strategies in class. Little did they know, they were focusing on the test and testing strategies every day. We wrote, we debated, we dissected documents, interpreted historical arguments, and just enjoyed learning about history--in some of the most unconventional ways at times. Behind closed doors, I was always researching ways to improve the course and my teaching strategies. I was also conducting informal assessments and keeping up with data and from the results, making modifications. When a student asked, "so, when are we going to start prepping for the test," I would reply, "we started prepping long ago, don't worry...you got this, the test is easier than you think." While I relaxed their minds, I never relaxed my standards, nor did I relax the rigor of the course. I also made my expectations clear, so we had a common goal that we were trying to accomplish. But I never eased up when the going got tough on either side. I am not going to lie and say as a result of my strategy, the majority of my students passed the Advanced Placement Exam. I can say that our campus saw significant gains in the number of students taking and passing the AP exam.

Students who never believed they were capable of passing such an exam displayed that they were nearly college-ready or above being labeled as "college-ready." I never viewed myself as an "AP Teacher" or teacher of "AP Students." I was a teacher who taught an AP Course to students taking an AP Course. I never lowered the bar or deviated from the College Board's standards for the course. I just changed my mindset and how I viewed the course. I closed the door and got my teaching on. A famous proverb says: as a man thinketh, so is he. We changed the way we thought about the course and became what the course wanted us to be. We kicked butt and demonstrated that we mastered the skills required of the course. My students had the potential; it was my goal to remove the intimidation. Removing the intimidation allowed them to perform at a level that many deemed as impossible.

We have to change the way we think about high expectations, especially rigor, when it comes to educating students in urban schools. It is possible to have high expectations, high campus and classroom standards, and a rigorous curriculum and students--ALL students--still succeed. Once again, the problem is not with the student. The problem is with us educators. When we change our perceptions about what students--especially students of color or low socio-economic status--can do, they will do it. Not merely because you told them they could, but you showed them how and supported them in the process. Because you wholeheartedly believed it, they achieved it.

## College and Career Ready

I took all the exams, filled out all the necessary applications, and submitted my FAFSA. When I got my official acceptance letter from Grambling State University, my heart dropped. I could not believe that I was going off to college. I was holding the exit ticket needed to get out of South Central, Los Angeles, finally, and do something different. In the Fall of 2004, I stepped foot on the campus of Grambling State University as the first in my family to graduate from high school and enroll in a four-year university. I did not feel 100% ready to be a college student--academic wise--but mentally, I was college-ready. College was not easy for me. I fought a lot of uphill battles. The main one was becoming a mom at the age of 20, right at the beginning of the Spring semester of my Sophomore year. I'll never forget when I called home and told my uncle that I was pregnant. He responded with three options: get an abortion, come back or send my baby home, or figure it out. I refused to get an abortion or send my son to Los Angeles to grow up in chaos and confusion. I had no choice but to figure it out 1, 686 miles from home. I got a night-shift job to provide for my son and took a full-load of classes during the day. Reflecting, it was at that moment that I realized I was more "college and career ready" than I thought.

More recently, College and Career Readiness (you might also see College, Career, and Military Readiness) have become the buzzwords of education. Educators are pushed, at all levels, to prepare students who are ready for college, a career, or the military branch after high school. Educators are internalizing CCRM readiness as exposure to colleges and career opportunities at an early age. CCRM readiness is also promoted through college-level classes at a secondary level and a surge in the usage of technology to prepare students to take on the 21st-century workforce. Curriculums are being redesigned to incorporate the opportunities for students to strengthen their written and oral communication skills, collaborate with others across networks, demonstrate creativity, and think critically in the classroom. We are giving students one test after another. The pressure is being placed on students to know exactly where they want to go to college and what career they want to have by the time they graduate high school. Those are encouraging strides towards equipping students for the future. But, is that really what it means to be "college and career ready"? Or, are we just extending this rat race to nowhere and adding unnecessary stress on students that they are not mentally prepared to handle?

In my opinion, College and Career Readiness is more about a mentality than it is about skills. Our students are leaving our schools with their brains packed and full of information. They possess various skills that will make them marketable but lack the mental grit required to stand firm when the going gets tough. For this reason, we see high depression rates and an increase in college drop-outs and poor job performances from some of the brightest students out there. They crammed all of the content knowledge required in their heads and learned all the skills we deemed necessary for the "21st century." But, when life began to stack up, they could not handle it. In the survival of the fittest society, on paper, they appeared to be healthy, but mentally they could not keep up with the demands of the most suitable.

We should continue to promote various college and career options to our students, require rigor in our courses, and provide students with every opportunity to learn new skills and trades. However, in doing so, we cannot and must not forget to provide opportunities for our students to learn, practice, and master what Jackie Gerstein (2013) refers to as the "Other 21st Century Skills." Tony Wagner, the author of *Creating Innovators,* asserts these other skills are necessary to face the challenges of the future. Such skills are agility and adaptability, initiative and entrepreneurship, perseverance, resilience, empathy and global stewardship, vision, and self-regulation. These skills are missing from today's education system. Sadly, we have students who leave our classrooms and schools who cannot and will not survive the direction our society and fast-paced culture is moving. There is hope, however, especially when it comes to teaching students in urban schools. This hope comes from me knowing, for a fact, that the "other 21st century skills" are in them. We have to show them what those skills look like in an academic and professional setting. We must also guide them in activating those skills while operating outside the walls of our schools and classrooms.

After I gave birth to my son during college, I was able to bounce back so quickly because the grind and hustle were already in me. Growing up in South Central--like many inner-city communities--you learn situational awareness and how to survive. I did not know what that looked like with the education system until it was broken down to me, and I was put in academic situations to sink or swim. If I wanted to get out of South

Central and do something that no one in my family had done before, I had no choice but to swim. I had to learn how to think fast on my feet and adapt as my surroundings and social settings began to change. If I wanted something to happen in my life, I had to make it happen for myself and could not rely on others to make it happen for me. When I could finally see past my obstacle, I started visioneering a future that *was* possible for me, and I went after it. It got to a point where my hustle was no longer about me but about the fact that I had two younger brothers who were looking up to me. If I was going to show them what they could do, I had to do it. I came from a broken community that believed the only real option in life was to become a product of our environment. I had to make a choice not to feed into that belief. There were moments when family and friends tried to pull me down and suck me back into their despair. But it was on me to check myself and fight to change the course of my life. When put in a situation where I needed to tap into my inner potential, I dug deep and brought it out. Our students have it in them already; we have to show them how to bring it out. Push them hard, make them sweat, and force them to show you their skills. They can and will do it. Don't let up.

When I entered college, I was not what many educators believe is "college and career ready." I had a low high school GPA, low ACT score, and was placed in remediation classes for math and reading. I was on "conditional acceptance" until I proved my academic potential. I also had no real knowledge of how to work a computer or navigate the Internet because my only access to both was when I was at school. And, to top it all off, I got pregnant twice--losing one to a miscarriage after a fight in my dorm hall--well before I started my sophomore year. These were the cards I received, and it was now on me to play my hand smart. I could not and refused to go home; finishing college was more significant to me once I became a mother. I had two eyes looking up at me, and I had to show my son how to handle life when the odds are against you. It was not easy, but I did it. I did it without missing a beat. After spending four years at Grambling State University, on May 16, 2008, I became the first in my family to receive a four-year college degree. I attribute what I was able to accomplish in life to the grace of God, and the values passed down to me by my late grandmother and late uncle. The street skills I developed as a result of growing up in the hood and strategies used to reach me by passionate educators also prepared me for that season of life.

## The Power of Going Back and Giving Back

We can acquire all of the knowledge and wealth in the world. However, if we choose to do nothing with it for the greater good of others, that wealth and education mean nothing. I am a firm believer that every being must see themselves as a vessel of change. They must make it their responsibility to go back and give back to their communities. Even if they have not physically left their neighborhood, whatever knowledge, experiences, or resources they have received, they must take back to the places they know as home. They should use the tools we have been entrusted with to promote change. In urban communities, there does not exist one standard understanding or definition for what it means to return to one's community of upbringing and "give back."

In 2005, Michelle A. Charles published a study titled *Giving Back to The Community: African American Inner-City Teens and Civic Engagement.* From her work, I have concluded that it is educators' responsibility to help our students develop a working definition of what it truly means to "give back." We must help them understand that giving back has more to do with actually doing than merely having a thought or an idea. Throughout this book, I have discussed the responsibility of educators to provide meaningful and relevant opportunities for students in urban schools. As it relates to the curriculum, we must guide them in identifying and solving issues that plague their communities. My reason is many of our students have witnessed what the idea of "giving back" looks like. However, they have to connect to doing the work of giving back. To youth in urban communities, "giving back" is something that they hear discussed by the elders, see it initiated by the church, or is a steward responsibility of a community member who "made it." They struggle with seeing themselves as a vessel of "giving back" and bringing change to their communities. Based on the research of Michelle A. Charles (2005), urban youth do not see a connection between "giving back" and their civic duties. To them, the two concepts have no connection. Students not being able to make this connection is one fault of the education system. Students are not being taught their responsibilities to their communities, nations, and the world.

When teaching our students what it looks like to return to their communities and give back, we must challenge the belief that their efforts, despite the size, will not be in vain. We must show them that "giving back" is not an adult-exclusive environment or an extension of faith organizations or non-profit groups. When educating and teaching our students what it means to "give back" to their communities, we must also be mindful of disconnecting our efforts with the efforts of the neighborhood. Instructing students on the various ways they can "give back" to their community starts in our classrooms but must go through the proper channels. As Charles' research uncovered, adults and elders in the communities are the "gatekeepers" of the communities. They are the ones that our urban youth look up to, take advice from, and model their ways after. If we are going to successfully create students who see "giving back" as an extension of their civic duties, then we must go through the proper channels. I have witnessed a disconnect between schools and communities. When parents are solicited to be involved in things happening in the school, the school dictates this involvement. Often, participation is limited to parent-teacher associations, booster clubs, or soliciting a parent chaperon or serving as a teacher's aide. I have seen attempts made by school districts to obtain feedback from parents on various issues. They use surveys and board meetings to speak to parents. But, I have yet to hear about or see a school go out into the community and genuinely ask community members how the school could be of service to them. The school must do a better job of working with all members of the community. Not just the members who have reached a certain level of status. This relationship is vital if any efforts to truly get students to "give back" and serve their communities will be successful.

So, where can you start when it comes to influencing students' under-standing of what it means to "give back?" First, you must begin with understanding their individual cultural beliefs and definitions of what it means to "go back and give back." Then you must know how their culture views and assumes their various civic duties. Understanding one's civic duty should not only be focused on at a primary level or isolated to social studies curriculum, but must happen continuously throughout one's schooling and be focused on--consistently--inside the classroom as well as at the campus level. We must be responsible for discussing what one's civic duties are. We must be sure to show the connection between public responsibilities and giving back. And, we should be mindful of students' views and the potential influences that shape their opinions when it comes to an understanding of their civic duties. This experience should not be an opportunity to promote political beliefs and agendas, although we do have a responsibility to support students in building their own socio-political consciousness and correct any deficit thinking that oppresses others. We must be sincere in our efforts to help our students understand they can individually and collec-tively transform their communities.

After students have linked "giving back" to their civic responsibilities, we should help them to understand how they can give back to their commu-nities. It is great to see community elders, religious organizations, and nonprofits leading the initiative of giving back. However, we want students to see there are things that they can do to give back, and they can start doing those things now. They do not have to wait until they have "made it out" to return and promote change in communities. They can begin setting examples of promoting change immediately. If they want to see a change happen in their community, that change can start with them. Despite what some may believe, people who live in urban communities are not content with their conditions. They see some things such as quality housing, access to quality foods, and political decisions made as out of their control. In our schools, we must show them that there are many things, both big and small, that they can do to bring about a change and the community they envision.

Once our students understand what it means to go back and give back, we must lead the way. With the assistance of the community, we must take them out to do the necessary work. But this effort must be one that is also done genuinely and takes place after we have made efforts to build trust and solid rapport with members of the community. No community or individual wants to feel as if it is a charity case (or a media opportunity) no matter how pure one's intentions might be. It will be a turn-off and possible road to conflict if we initiate community trans-formation projects without the input or involvement of the community. After we have gotten the community on board, create opportunities for students to go out and do. While doing, your role is to put your hands to work, monitor, and support. When students return to the classroom, follow-up with them, and help them develop action plans to continue what they have started. As well, acknowledge and congratulate them on their individual and collective efforts--both inside and outside of the classroom. We want to bring awareness to their efforts and spark flames in the minds of others. If the school is on board and all in, that is great. But the goal is to get the school and the community in on the action of giving back. We want to build a stable bridge that connects the school and community.

Some of my most transformative years as an educator happened during my very first years in the profession. I learned what it meant to call myself a teacher truly. I also learned the great responsibility that I had--as a person who "made it"--to those who it was my duty to educate. As shared in a previous chapter, I started my teaching career in a small majority-black school district. This school district, like any school district, had its share of obstacles. But it also had a great deal of success that is still evident to this day. One achievement that stood out to me about the school district and the community was how people gave back. They knew the possibilities that awaited and wanted to play whatever role they could to ensure that future generations also had a shot at "making it."

Many students do not get the opportunity to witness "success stories" return to their campus or community to help students write their own success stories. However, with the influence we possess as educators, we must fight to change this. It is common for students from urban communities to be told "get out of here and never come back"--I was one of them. But we must change this because there are students out there who need to see people who have been in their shoes, and have made it out, come back to lend them a helping hand. If we cannot physically return to the communities and schools where it all started, we must situate ourselves in communities that are similar to our own and fight. Education and the resources we have at our disposal will serve as our weapons to give back in any way possible. There is a great privilege in tutoring kids in the community, coaching local little leagues, or even just returning to schools to read a book or give words of hope. These actions can make a difference in the lives of someone who is looking for an example to follow. Our students should see themselves as those current and future examples.

In our classrooms and schools, we can show our students that there are ways to escape their current conditions and environments. But never stop encouraging them to go back and change those conditions and situations that once held them back. Imagine the transformation that would happen if educators, doctors, lawyers, politicians, store owners, clergymen, etc. returned and did the real work to restore urban spaces where they once lived. It would give a new life and a new hope to those young hearts who can't envision what "success" looks like because they have never seen it done or have been told there's only one way to be successful. Early on, we must provide our students with every opportunity to envision themselves as their definition of success and community transformer. But this transformation does not start in communities. It begins when we pull students off the ledge and help them realize the real potential that lies within them.

## Classroom Strategies for Preparing Students for What They Can Be

**My Dream Resume**: Similar to a vision board, having students design a dream resume--for a future profession or research activity related to their ideal career--is a great way to plan for the future. We must expose students to creating resumes and using resumes to highlight their strengths early in their education. Many students leave high school, not knowing what a resume looks like or even how to put one together. As a result, they miss out on many job opportunities that they are already qualified to obtain. In addition to preparing a resume, it is also vital that we show students how to use a resume as a selling tool and teach them the importance of first impressions. As well, practicing interview skills with students is also essential, inside and outside of the classroom. Never pass up the opportunity to have your students practice resume building, elevator pitches, and interviewing skills. If we are going to prepare them for the future, we must start today.

**Game Changers**: Numerous apps exist that allow students to see what the future holds for them based on the good, risky, and bad decisions that they make. What I like most about these apps is that they expose students to real scenarios and what could be real outcomes if they make poor choices. It also provides an excellent opportunity for students to understand the importance of situational awareness and how one wrong move can be detrimental to one's future. Bring this concept into our classrooms, have your students design simulation and games surrounding the idea of decision making. In doing so, allow them to design what the game will look like, the rules of the game, and how various scenarios and situations combined will shape the outcome of the game. Games, as such, are easy to design around content--like math monopoly--and can serve as a great follow-up to a lesson or a tool to engage students when downtime exists. With anything, reflection after the creation and application stages are essential in making sure students connect learning experiences and content with their reality. No matter how you implement this strategy into your classroom, give your students a shot at changing the game, especially if they can see how they have the power to change their lives.

**If I Ruled the World**: If you ruled the world, what would you do with your new power and influence? If you had the opportunity to change anything, what would it be? Would you change it for good, or would you change it for the bad? Asking students what they would do if they ruled the world can be adapted to fit our classroom in many ways. You can use this strategy as an introduction activity as a way to practice debates, a segue to a problem-solution project, a great way to practice speech writing and public speaking, or as a simple, quick write or reflection activity. Most importantly, asking students what they would do if they ruled the world is a good way to help students realize, and possibly *actualize* the agency they possess and the power they have in shaping the outcomes of their lives. Although many students do not envision themselves as every having power or influence over the world, posing the simple question--in whatever fashion you choose--is an excellent strategy for getting students to think beyond what they can currently see.

**Catch 'Em And Skill Them In**: We need to make sure that our students are leaving our classrooms and schools with knowledge and know-how of every skill out there. From how to prepare and send a professional email, putting together a professional presentation, to even how to create and stick to a budget. If it is a skill, they need to know to be successful in the future, and in life, we have to teach them those skills. There are many certifications that our students can obtain to prepare them for college and the workforce. Various community opportunities can expose our students to what will give them the necessary life skills they will need to survive after high school. Whether we help students get a Google Certification, Microsoft Office Certification, or bring a local financial expert to show them how to open a checking or savings account and balance a checkbook, a part of preparing our students for the future requires us, now, to catch 'em and skill them in with every opportunity we get.

**Community Partnerships**: The success of the community is a direct extension of the success of the schools in the community. Schools and districts cannot function or thrive in isolation of one another. If a business is in the community, then our students should be involved in the success of our business. What partnership does your school have with the community? How can you and your students strengthen those existing partnerships or create new connections? As discussed in this chapter, we have to show our students that they are a significant part of their community. Because of this, they should be active in shaping and developing their communities. Through your content and problem-solution projects, help your students get out and get involved in their communities. They can do this through partnerships and bonds that will bring the communities and schools closer to one another.

NINE

# REFLECTION

---

*"Eight hours in a day is all we need to show our students real love."*

ME

---

My core belief is that students in urban schools deserve teachers who are willing to get REAL with them and show them an unfailing love. If you are a teacher in an urban school, or any school for that matter, and you are not willing or ready to show REAL LOVE to your students, then get out because you are doing more harm to them than you are doing any good. I was one of those students who was fortunate enough to experience educators from both sides. I had educators who couldn't care less if I was successful or not, and I had educators who believed I could and would defy the odds. I had educators who sold me the fatalistic belief that I came from nothing and, as a result, was destined to be nothing. Then, others saw and helped me bring out the best that was already in me. Because I know how it feels to be told and shown that you are nothing and I know how it feels to be informed about and proved your worth, I have no choice but to use my story--my testimony--to help other students who are walking the same path that I journey.

Educators played a prominent role in shaping who I am today; a person who defied the odds against them. Someone invested in me, so I must invest in others. The work I do, as an educator, is transformative. Because I cannot personally save every student in every urban school, I have made it my duty to reform urban schools through the educators who work in urban schools. REAL LOVE is higher than me and, again, is more than just some catchy acronym. It is a call to educators around the world to realize the power we possess to make or break a student. It is a call for educators to wake up and realize that there are students, who have succumbed to fatalism, and because they feel unloved and unworthy, they are standing on the edge, ready to jump. They entered our buildings with their flashlights on and made numerous cries for help, but their lights met faces that were blind, and their calls fell on death ears. They can't take it anymore. And, why should they even try when our society has stacked the odds against them?

Every student has the potential to become a success story despite what we may see now. However, their understanding and visions of success start in our schools and classrooms. We possess more power and influence than we think over the lives of our students, but we must first believe this to be accurate and ready to do some necessary work. I heard that the most significant problem educators faced was that we only had our students for eight hours a day, and society had them for the remaining sixteen. However, I disagree with this contention because I know and have experienced the power of the eight. For eight hours a day (and sometimes even more), we can love, inspire, uplift, support, guide, and influence. We have the power to help students envision and preserve, but we have to be willing to get down in the mud with them when the going gets tough. For eight hours a day, we have the power to help students see their potential, plan for the future, and support them in transforming their communities. We can design amazing lessons that make students get it, show them value in their communities, and be there when there is nothing else we can do.

We have the power to show our students how to take back their shame and turn their vulnerabilities into courage. We can create game-changers, thinkers, doers, innovators, and every other career imaginable. Eight hours a day is all we need because when you add those hours up, we come out on top with approximately 20,000 hours to show our students R.E.A.L. L.O.V.E, transform lives, and help them blaze their paths when they see no way out. Some excellent educators, throughout our lives, used their eight hours to grab hold of us and capture our hearts so we must do the same. No! We can and will do the same, and it starts now with understanding the power-packed into our eight. It's time to do some necessary and transformative work. It's about time that we start getting REAL with ours and let our LOVE for them lead the way.

# REFERENCES

Adichie, C. N. (2009, July). *The Danger of a Single Story*. Retrieved October 20, 2019, from https://www.ted.com/talks.

Barbour, C. (1993). Integrating the Curriculum v1 [Video]. Virginia, USA: Association for Supervision and Curriculum Development.

Bilyeu, Clint (2018, July 16). Playing It Safe is Dangerous. Here's Why [Video File]. Retrieved from https://www.youtube.com/watch?v=1xxegA6MLY8&t=318s

Brown, A. H., Cervero, R. M., & Johnson-Bailey, J. (2000). Making the Invisible Visible: Race, Gender, and Teaching in Adult Education. Adult Education Quarterly, 50(4), 273–288. https://doi.org/10.1177/074171360005000402

*Brene Brown on Empathy*. (2013). Retrieved from
   https://youtu.be/1Evwgu369Jw

Brown, B. (2011, January 3). *The Power of
   Vulnerability*. Retrieved from YouTube: https://
   www.youtube.com/watch?v=iCvmsMzlF7o

Brown, B. (2017, April 7). *Daring Classrooms*.
   Retrieved from YouTube:
   https://www.youtube.com/watch?
   v=DVD8YRgA-ck.

Brown, D. (2019, May 2). 'Yeet???' High School
   Teacher Creates 'Gen Z Dictionary' of all the
   terms students use. Retrieved from https://
   www.usatoday.com/story/tech/2019/05/01/
   take-notes-cool-teacher-made-list-slang-terms-
   gen-z-students-use/3640898002/

Burney, L. (2019, January 17). What freedom feels
   like to Nipsey Hussle. Retrieved from
   https://www.thefader.com/2019/01/17/what-
   freedom-feels-like-to-nipsey-hussle.

Canfield, J. (2017, September 28). *How to Find Your
   Purpose in Life* [Video File]. Retrieved from
   https://www.youtube.com/watch?
   v=z8XECSIoEgE

Chapman, G. D. (2017). *The 5 Love Languages: The
   Secret to Love That Lasts*. Vereeniging: Christian
   Art Publishers.

Charles, M. M. (2005). Giving Back to The Community: African American Inner City Teens and Civic Engagement. *Circle Working Paper 38*, 2–34.

Delpit, L., Kohl, H., Lesesne, P., & Payne, C. M. (2006). *Other People's Children: Cultural Conflict in the Classroom*. New York: New Press.

Douglas, T.-R. M., & Nganga, C. W. (2015). Radical Loving, Radical Leading: Negotiating Complex Identities, Positionalities, and Pedagogy in Social Justice Work. In C. Boske, & A. F. Osanloo, *Living the Work: Promoting Social Justice and Equity Work in Schools Around the World* (pp. 59-86). Bingley: Emerald Group Publishing Limited.

Drake, S.M. & Joanne, L.R. (2018). Integrated Curriculum as an Effective Way to Teach 21st Century Capabilities. Journal of Educational Research, 1(1), pp.31-50.

Emdin, C. (2011). Moving Beyond the Boat without a Paddle: Reality Pedagogy, Black Youth, and Urban Science Education. *The Journal of Negro Education, 80*(3), 284-295. Retrieved May 13, 2020, from www.jstor.org/stable/41341134

Emdin, C. (2012, August 23). *Reality Pedagogy: Christopher Emdin at TedxTeachersCollege* [Video File]. Retrieved from https://www.youtube.com/watch?v=2Y9tVf_8fqo

Emdin, C. (2013, March 7). *Empowering Children Through Urban Education: Christopher Emdin at TedxColumbiaSIPA* [Video File]. Retrieved from https://www.youtube.com/watch?v=ouudXr-csZg

Emdin, C. (2016, September). Seven Cs for Effective Teaching. Retrieved from http://www.ascd.org/publications/educational-leadership/sept16/vol74/num01/Seven-Cs-for-Effective-Teaching.aspx.

Emdin, C. (2016). *For White Folks Who Teach in the Hood ... and the Rest of Y'all Too: Reality Pedagogy and Urban Education*. Boston: Beacon Press.

Emdin, C. (2017, March 6). *We Got It from Here...Thank You for Your Service* [Video File]. Retrieved from https://www.youtube.com/watch?v=XbBwM1c-6xM&t=2786s

Emdin, C. (2018, March 6). *Teaching & Being Rachetdemic* [Video File]. Retrieved from https://www.youtube.com/watch?v=4QmFREcXri0.

Fay, L. (2019, August 7). 74 Interview: Researcher Gloria Ladson-Billings on Culturally Relevant Teaching, the Role of Teachers in Trump's America & Lessons from Her Two Decades in Education Research. Retrieved from https://www.the74million.org/article/74-interview-researcher-gloria-ladson-billings-on-culturally-relevant-teaching-the-role-of-teachers-in-trumps-america-lessons-from-her-two-decades-in-education-research/.

Finley, R. (2013, February). *A Guerrilla Gardener in South Central LA*. Retrieved from https://www.ted.com/talks/ron_finley_a_guerilla_gardener_in_south_central_la?language=en

Finley, T. (2017, July 12). Angela Rye Has A New Podcast for The Woke and 'Spohistiratchet': Rye discusses blackness, politics, current events, and more on "On One."

Feld, L. D., & Shusterman, A. (2015). Into the pressure cooker: Student stress in college preparatory high schools. *Journal of Adolescence,41*, 31-42. doi:10.1016/j.adolescence.2015.02.003

Gay, G. (2018). *Culturally Responsive Teaching: Theory, Research, and Practice. Multicultural Education Series*. Teachers College Press.

Gerstein, J. The Other 21st Century Skills. (2016, November 5). Retrieved from https://usergeneratededucation.wordpress.com/2013/05/22/the-other-21st-century-skills/

Hammond, Z., & Jackson, Y. (2015). *Culturally Responsive Teaching and The Brain: Promoting Authentic Engagement and Rigor Among Culturally and Linguistically Diverse Students*. Thousand Oaks, CA: Corwin, a SAGE Company.

Howard, G. R. (1999). *We Can't Teach What We Don't Know: White Teachers, Multiracial Schools. Multicultural Education Series*. Teachers College Press.

Jarrett, Olga S., and Vera Stenhouse. "Problem Solution Project." *Urban Education*, vol. 46, no. 6, 2011, pp. 1461–1495., doi:10.1177/0042085911400336.

King, Patricia M., and Karen Strohm-Kitchener. *Developing Reflective Judgment: Understanding and Promoting Intellectual Growth and Critical Thinking in Adolescents and Adults*. Jossey-Bass Publishers, 1994.

Ladson-Billings, G. (1995). But That's Just Good Teaching! The Case for Culturally Relevant Pedagogy. *Theory into Practice*, 159-165.

Ladson-Billings, G. (2006). From the Achievement Gap to the Education Debt: Understanding Achievement in U.S. Schools. *Educational Researcher*, 3–12.

Ladson-Billings, G. (2007). *The Dream Keepers: Successful Teachers of African American Children.* San Francisco: John Wiley & Sons, Inc.

Maher, F.A., & Tetreault, M.K. (1993). Frames of Positionality: Constructing meaningful dialogues about gender and race. *Anthropological Quarterly, 66*(3), 118-126.

Moody. (n.d.). 5 Love Language Profiles. Retrieved from https://www. 5lovelanguages.com/quizzes/.

Milner, H. R. (2012). Rethinking Achievement Gap Talk in Urban Education. *Urban Education,* 3–8.

New Line Productions. (1995). *Friday.*

Pang, V. O. (2018). *Diversity & Equity in the Classroom.* Boston, MA: Cengage Learning.

Schön, D. A. (1983). *The reflective practitioner: How professionals think in action.* New York: Basic Books.

Shakur, T. (1999). *Selected poems from the rose that grew from concrete.* New York: Scholastic.

Sinek, S. (2011). *Start with Why: How Great Leaders Inspire Everyone to Take Action.* London: Portfolio Penguin.

Smith, C. (2014, July). The Danger of Silence.

Tony Wagner's Seven Survival Skills. (n.d.).
    Retrieved from http://www.tonywagner.com/7-
    survival-skills/

V. A. & Congdon, J. (Directors). (2009). A Race to
    Nowhere [Video file]. United States: Reel Links
    Film.

*Victory Lap.* (n.d.). Interscope Studios.

Wonders, H. (n.d.). Does Talking to Plants Help
    Them Grow? Retrieved from https://www.
    wonderopolis.org/wonder/does-talking-to-
    plants-help-them-grow.

# ABOUT THE AUTHOR

Alexes M. Terry is a wife, mom, educator, and founder of TwistED Teaching Educational Consulting Company. Using her ten years of experience in Education, she mentors, coaches, and consults educators who work with students in urban schools and communities. Through TwistED Teaching, her overall goal is to "twist the way we do teaching and learning in urban schools" by supporting educators in creating learning environments and opportunities that are equitable, culturally relevant, and responsive, engaging, and meets the diverse needs of all students.

# OTHER EDUMATCH TITLES

*EduMatch Snapshot in Education (2016)*
*In this collaborative project, twenty educators located throughout the United States share educational strategies that have worked well for them, both with students and in their professional practice.*

*The #EduMatch Teacher's Recipe Guide*
**Editors: Tammy Neil & Sarah Thomas**
*Dive in as fourteen international educators share their recipes for success, both literally and metaphorically!*

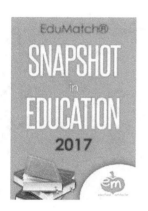

*EduMatch Snapshot in Education (2017)*
*We're back! EduMatch proudly presents Snapshot in Education (2017). In this two-volume collection, 32 educators and one student share their tips for the classroom and professional practice.*

*Journey to The "Y" in You* by Dene Gainey
*This book started as a series of separate writing pieces that were eventually woven together to form a fabric called The Y in You. The question is, "What's the 'why' in you?"*

*The Teacher's Journey* by Brian Costello
*Follow the Teacher's Journey with Brian as he weaves together the stories of seven incredible educators. Each step encourages educators at any level to reflect, grow, and connect.*

*The Fire Within*
Compiled and edited by Mandy Froehlich
*Adversity itself is not what defines us. It is how we react to that adversity and the choices we make that creates who we are and how we will persevere.*

*EduMagic* by Sam Fecich
*This book challenges the thought that "teaching" begins only after certification and college graduation. Instead, it describes how students in teacher preparation programs have value to offer their future colleagues, even as they are learning to be teachers!*

*Makers in Schools*
Editors: Susan Brown & Barbara Liedahl
*The maker mindset sets the stage for the Fourth Industrial Revolution,*
*empowering educators to guide their students.*

*Divergent EDU* by Mandy Froehlich
*The concept of being innovative can be made to sound so simple. But what if the*
*development of the innovative thinking isn't the only roadblock?*

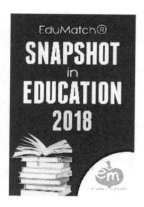

*EduMatch Snapshot in Education (2018)*
*EduMatch® is back for our third annual Snapshot in Education. Dive in as 21*
*educators share a snapshot of what they learned, what they did, and how they*
*grew in 2018.*

Daddy's Favorites by Elissa Joy
Illustrated by Dionne Victoria
*Five-year-old Jill wants to be the center of everyone's world. But, her most*
*favorite person in the world, without fail, is her Daddy. But Daddy has to be*
*Daddy, and most times that means he has to be there when everyone needs him,*
*especially when her brother Danny needs him.*

*Level Up Leadership* by Brian Kulak
*Gaming has captivated its players for generations and cemented itself as a fundamental part of our culture. In order to reach the end of the game, they all need to level up.*

*DigCit Kids* edited by Marialice Curran & Curran Dee
*This book is a compilation of stories, starting with our own mother and son story, and shares examples from both parents and educators on how they embed digital citizenship at home and in the classroom.*

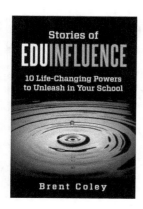

*Stories of EduInfluence* by **Brent Coley**
*In Stories of EduInfluence, veteran educator Brent Coley shares stories from more than two decades in the classroom and front office.*

*The Edupreneur* by **Dr. Will**
*The Edupreneur is a 2019 documentary film that takes you on a journey into the successes and challenges of some of the most recognized names in K-12 education consulting.*

*In Other Words* by Rachelle Dene Poth

*In Other Words is a book full of inspirational and thought-provoking quotes that have pushed the author's thinking and inspired her.*

*To Whom it May Concern*
Editors: Sarah-Jane Thomas, PhD & Nicol R. Howard, PhD

*In To Whom it May Concern..., you will read a collaboration between two Master's in Education classes at two universities on opposite coasts of the United States.*

*One Drop of Kindness* by Jeff Kubiak
*This children's book, along with each of you, will change our world as we know it. It only takes One Drop of Kindness to fill a heart with love.*

*Differentiated Instruction in the Teaching Profession* by Kristen Koppers
*Differentiated Instruction in the Teaching Profession is an innovative way to use critical thinking skills to create strategies to help all students succeed. This book is for educators of all levels who want to take the next step into differentiating their instruction.*

*L.E.A.D. from Day One* by Ryan McHale
*L.E.A.D. from Day One is a go-to resource to help educators outline a future plan toward becoming a teacher leader. The purpose of this book is to help you see just how easily you can transform your entire mindset to become the leader your students need you to be.*

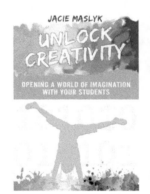

*Unlock Creativity* by Jacie Maslyk
*Every classroom is filled with creative potential. Unlock Creativity will help you discover opportunities that will make every student see themselves as a creative thinker.*

*Make Waves!* by Hal Roberts

*In Make Waves! Hal discusses 15 attributes of a great leader. He shares his varied experience as a teacher, leader, a player in the N.F.L., and a plethora of research to take you on a journey to emerge as leader of significance.*

*21 Lessons of Tech Integration Coaching* by Martine Brown

*In 21 Lessons of Tech Integration Coaching, Martine Brown provides a practical guide about how to use your skills to support and transform schools.*

*Everyone Can Learn Math* by Alice Aspinall

*How do you approach a math problem that challenges you? Do you keep trying until you reach a solution? Or are you like Amy, who gets frustrated easily and gives up?*

*EduMagic Shine On* by Sam Fecich, Katy Gibson, Hannah Sansom, and Hannah Turk

*EduMagic: A Guide for New Teachers picks up where EduMagic: A Guide for Preservice Teachers leaves off. Dr. Sam Fecich is back at the coffee shop and is now joined by three former students-turned-friends. She is excited to introduce you to these three young teachers: Katy Gibson, Hannah Sansom, and Hannah Turk.*

*Unconventional* by Rachelle Dene Poth
*Unconventional will empower educators to take risks, explore new ideas and emerging technologies, and bring amazing changes to classrooms. Dive in to transform student learning and thrive in edu!*

*All In* by Kristen Nan & Jacie Maslyk
*Unlike Nevada's slogan of "what happens in Vegas, stays in Vegas," this book reminds us that what happens in the classroom, should never stay within the classroom!*

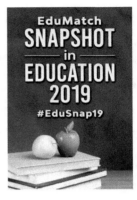

*EduMatch Snapshot in Education 2019*
*EduMatch® is back for our fourth annual Snapshot in Education. Dive in as an international crew of educators share a snapshot of what they learned, what they did, and how they grew in 2019. Topics include Social Emotional Learning, identity, instructional tips, and much more!*

*Play? Yay!* by BreAnn Fennell
*Play? Yay! is a book my mom wrote for kids. I'm a toddler, and I like to read. I sit and look at pictures or point to my favorite pages. Do you like books like that? Then this book is for you too! The best part about this book is that you can read it with people like moms, dads, or grandparents. Get Play? Yay! today for fun, rhymes, and the gift of imagination.*

*The EdCorps Classroom* by Chris Aviles
*In this how-to guide, Chris Aviles tells you how he accidentally stumbled into the world of student-run businesses, and how you can use them to provide authentic learning to your students.*

*Strive* by Robert Dunlop
*This book will get you thinking about how happy you are in your career and give you practical strategies to make changes that will truly impact your happiness.*

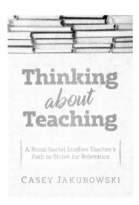

*Thinking About Teaching* by Casey Jakubowski

*This book explores the thoughts that author Casey T. Jakubowski, PhD has on a wide range of education related topics. Seeking to give voice to rural education, in this unstable time, and reflecting on a wide of research and experiences, this work offers all educators, from the beginning, all the way to the end, a reflective voice to channel their own experiences against and with on their journey.*

*I'm Sorry Story* by Melody McAllister

*Do you know what it's like to sit by yourself at lunch? Do you know how it feels when it seems everyone around you has close friends except you? That's exactly how Ryan feels. He wants good friends and he wants to be accepted by his classmates, but he isn't sure how to make that happen. Join him as he learns to put others first and make things right when he has been wrong!*

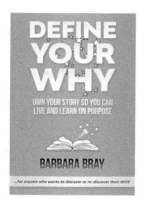

*Define Your Why* by Barbara Bray
*Barbara Bray wrote Define Your WHY from the process she went through to figure out her WHY and through coaching others who did not feel valued, appreciated, or why they needed to live on purpose.*

*To the Edge* by Kyle Anderson
*From risks that resulted in immediate success to ones that elicited failure and regret, you surely will be inspired by Kyle's story. Take yourself to the edge and become more of a risk-taker in your life and career! #ToTheEdgeEDU*

*Systems, Cycles, Seasons, & Processes* by Emjay Smith
*Systems, Cycles, Seasons, and Processes takes you on a journey to discover the laws, concepts, and principles that govern the seen and unseen realms of life.*

*The Tiebreaker* by Rebecca Gibboney
*In The Tiebreaker, Rebecca Gibboney gives educators the scouting report on how to build a culture of gamification for professional learning.*

*Fur Friends Forever* by LaTezeon Humprey Balentine
*Follow this amazing adventure of two dogs with different lifestyles as they take on a new situation that tests them. This story is about friendship and all that comes with it including peer pressure in decision making.*

*The Perfect Puppy* by Kristen Koppers
*Many times we often judge others before we learn about them. Abbey Mae learns how it feels to not be accepted by others. Follow her journey as she finds out who she is on the inside.*

EduMatch Publishing